Acoustic Guitar

Printed and bound in the EU

Published by SMT, an imprint of Bobcat Books Limited,
14/15 Berners Street, London W1T 3LJ, UK

www.musicsales.com

Photographs courtesy of Carol Farnworth

Music typesetting by David Mead and Cambridge Notation

While the publishers have made every reasonable effort to trace the copyright owners
for any or all of the photographs in this book, there may be some omissions of
credits, for which we apologise.

ISBN 1-84492-031-3
SMT1012R

Acoustic Guitar

David Mead

BOOK CONTENTS

CD CONTENTS

Audio recorded and engineered by Martin Holmes at Sandpit Studios, Bath (martinholmes@ukonline.co.uk).

David Mead uses Yamaha acoustic guitars, a Yamaha AG Stomp acoustic preamp and Elixir strings.

Background music on Track 46 excerpted from the CD *Cloud Factory* by David Mead (see www.davidmead.net for details).

ABOUT THE AUTHOR

David Mead has been involved in playing and teaching the guitar for over 20 years. During that time he has edited both *Guitarist* and *Guitar Techniques* magazines and authored 12 books, which have enjoyed sales in excess of 100,000 worldwide.

David's playing career was sidetracked by private teaching during the 1980s and eventually by a career in journalism in the 1990s. He joined the writing team of UK magazine *Guitarist* in 1992 and was made editor in 1995. In 1996, he took over the editorship of *Guitar Techniques* magazine, where his teaching experience saw him develop the title into one of the world's most respected guitar tutorial monthlies.

In 2001, with the books *10 Minute Guitar Workout* and *100 Guitar Tips You Should Have Been Told* (also available from SMT) already on the bookshelves, he left the magazines behind to focus on his alternate career as an author and player. David currently contributes a column to *Guitar Techniques* and is a regular contributor to both *Guitarist* and *What Guitar?* magazines.

www.davidmead.net

ACKNOWLEDGEMENTS

As usual, I'd like to thank Carol for all the 'gentle encouragement' (I've still got the bruises) in this strange business called creativity. Also my children, Timothy and Toby, as ever.

Special thanks to Martin Holmes for being my chaperone in the recording studio. I'm not safe left alone with technology.

Finally, thanks to all at SMT for letting me do my thing without hindrance, and a very big tip of the hat to all the guitar mags who use my words.

INTRODUCTION

It's my contention that *Crash Course* is a bit of a brutal title for anything so inherently gentle as playing one of the greatest instruments on Earth. And the idea that I can turn you into a partly fledged musician in a mere two months might sound like stretching credibility somewhat, too. But this isn't some kind of military training school, and you haven't joined a highly specialised wing of the armed forces, so the pace is going to be a lot more gentle than you might be expecting.

I'm aware that modern life, even in the most 'normal' of domestic scenarios, can be a little chaotic, to say the least. I'm also aware that, in the scale of things, guitar practice isn't high on the list of anyone's priorities when there are other, more pressing matters to the fore, so I'm not going to insist that you stand in the corner if you miss a day or so here and there. I'm going to be realistic and merely ask that you give everything here your best shot.

After all, the deal between us is pretty straightforward: you want to learn to play acoustic guitar in the most direct way possible – not exactly cutting corners, but certainly taking all the short cuts available. Right? Well, I want that too, and so together we should make a pretty good team.

David Mead
2004

HOW IT WORKS

What you'll find inside this book is a strategy whereby I've laid out for you a lesson for every day of the week, with a test on every seventh day to tie together everything you've learned in that period. You should find most of the lessons quite easy as the gradient is not too demanding, especially at first. By the end of the book, you should be ready to go out into the wider world of acoustic-guitar playing with the foundations of your knowledge dug deep.

Whenever there's an example of exercise which is demonstrated by my own fair hand on the accompanying CD, you'll find this icon. It will help you to assimilate these tasks much quicker if you hear them played first, so make sure there's a CD player handy in your practice room.

Whenever there's an exercise which I think might not be as immediate as some of the others, I'll use this weightlifing icon. It implies that working at it over a length of time will build up the necessary stamina to let you push forward.

Sometimes you'll find an exercise that has to be completed in a set period of time – two minutes, for example. If this is the case, you'll find this particular symbol nearby. And you thought you'd never use that timer function on your wristwatch!

When I really want to make a point, I may resort to using an exclamation mark, like the one shown here. Don't think of it as me shouting – I don't do that kind of thing.

At the end of each week, you'll have a little test to complete and it will be heralded by this symbol. If you started the book on a Monday, you'll find yourself doing the tests on Sundays – you know, when you've got all that free time...

During my years as a guitar-magazine journalist, I got the chance to mingle with some of the top guitarists in the world. When you see these quote marks, it's usually because I've remembered something wise one of them said.

GETTING STARTED

The first thing we're going to do is learn a little geography. (That's guitar geography, obviously.) I'm going to be referring to your instrument's various bits and pieces by their accepted names, and it will save a lot of time if I don't have to stop and say, 'You know, that silver wiggly bit by the long black thing' each time. So, seeing as a picture saves me writing 1,000 words, take a look at this:

Basic guitar geography

The only other thing I'd ask you to do before we actually become embroiled, as it were, is to take a look at the finely crafted section called 'The Basics'. You don't need to read it all now – although I hope you do eventually (it took hours to write, y'know). It covers some of the questions that you'll find yourself wanting to ask before too long and gives you a bit of an extended insight into the instrument you're holding in your hands.

YOU'VE GOT MORE QUESTIONS?

I really hope that I'll be able to cover everything you'll need during the eight weeks we'll be spending together, but if I don't I like to offer a bit of a back-up service. If you've got a query about anything in this book, you're more than welcome to email me through my website at www.davidmead.net. I try to answer all the emails I receive, although I stop short of conducting correspondence courses online! So don't let anything bug you; if I can help, I will.

READING MUSIC

As you are undoubtedly unfamiliar with all the signs, terms and symbols used in music today, it's probably worth reading through this section before you try to make sense of any of the lessons. I don't expect you to remember it all at once, of course, and so be prepared to keep flicking back to check a few things out until you get the general hang of things after a while.

CHORD BOXES

Probably the first thing you'll come across in guitar notation is a chord box. This is a diagram that represents the guitar neck as a sort of grid:

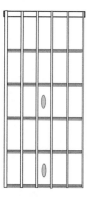

In the diagram on the left, the horizontal lines represent the guitar's frets, whilst the vertical lines represent the strings. The string on the far left is the thickest string on the guitar, known as the 'lowest string'. Many people think that this is slightly odd, because when you're holding the guitar it isn't really the 'lowest' string as such; in fact, it's the one that's closest to you. But the reason we call it this is owing to the fact that it's lowest in pitch. In other words, it's bassier than any of the other strings you've got.

If this sort of thing sounds confusing, then hang on to your hat because music – and guitar playing – is full of little quirky things like this. You'll soon fall into line, I assure you.

We give each of the strings the name of the note to which it's tuned. So this means that they go across the fretboard, left to right in the diagram, like this:

E A D G B E

So the thickest string nearest you is known as the E string. In fact, because there are two Es on the guitar, it's more commonly known as the *bass* or *lower* E. In the previous diagram, you'll notice that there is a thickish line across the top. This is known as the *nut*. It's the point where the fretboard begins and it does

the job of keeping the strings in place as they travel from their respective tuners, down along the fretboard and ending at the bridge.

The reason why it's known as the nut is lost in the vague mists of time. That's just what it's called – and I'm sure we're all far too grown up to argue about it.

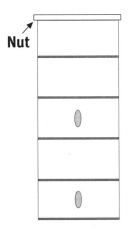

When you see that thick line at the top of a chord box, as shown on the left, you know that you're meant to be at the nut end of the fretboard. If you're actually meant to be somewhere further up, fear not because you'll have two big clues. One is that the thick line will disappear and the other is that I'll let you know by putting a number against the chord box to reorientate you, fret-wise.

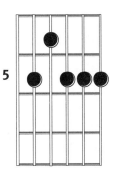

In the diagram on the right, the fret at the top of the box is the fifth – indicated by the number 5 on the left-hand side. We won't be venturing up this far for a while, but I always think that it's nice to know what lies in the future, don't you?

Back to the plot. The next thing to take a look at is where to put your fingers on the strings. Exactly how you do this is explained more fully in the lessons, and so I won't waste time examining it here. All you need to know for now is the general geography of the thing; we'll be addressing specifics quite soon. Take a look at this diagram:

Acoustic Guitar

C major

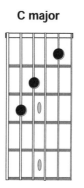

You've probably already guessed that the black blobs somehow represent your fingers – and you're dead right. Exactly which is which might still be puzzling you, though...

If you hold your left hand out in front of you, palm facing the floor, the fingers are numbered like this: working left from the thumb (the only finger here that's not used on the actual fretboard in common practice), we have finger 1, also known as the index finger; then finger 2, usually the longest finger on the hand; then 3, the ring finger; and finally the little finger, or 'pinkie' if you watch too many American soaps.

So, in the diagram at the top of the next page, you're being asked to place your first finger on the first fret, second string. Now, I know that this is going to involve an awful lot of looking to and from the book, your hand, the guitar neck and so on, but don't worry if this is something you find quite difficult to grasp in the very early stages. Just take your time; you'll find that you become familiar with this sort of diagram really quickly and will soon be blazing away on the guitar neck.

Have a close look at this arrangement, just to make sure this little bit of guitar-fretboard orienteering has got through:

C major

3 2 1

I don't want you to try to play this chord just yet – there's some additional information you'll need first in order to play it. Just look at it and work out which finger goes where.

If you've concluded that the first finger goes on the second string, first fret, the second finger on the fourth string, second fret, and the third finger goes on the fifth string, third fret, then reward yourself with something nice from that secret cache of chocolate we all know you've got hidden somewhere, because you're absolutely right.

As I've said, actually saying all this 'third finger on the second string' business might sound like a helluva long way of doing things, but it's necessary at the beginning. I promise you that you'll pick things up really quickly and you'll soon be able just to look at a chord box and play the chord pretty much immediately.

NOUGHTS AND CROSSES

There's really just one other thing that you ought to know about chord boxes for now, and this concerns the unfretted – or open – strings. Take another look at that chord box:

Acoustic Guitar

C major

3 2 1

We've worked out where the fingers go, but what about the strings without fingers on? Does this mean we include them in the chord? Or do we try to miss them out?

Never fear. This is where another helpful couple of indicators come in. In many guitar chords, you aren't expected to play all six strings – and if this is the case, you'll find a little 'x' over the relevant string, like this:

The x means that you miss this string out when you sound the chord. To begin with, most of the time you'll find that the 'missed out' strings are on the bottom (remember, these are the ones nearest to you when you're holding the guitar in a playing position), and so they're pretty easy to miss out. However, if the reverse is true and you're actually meant to include them in the chord, you'll find a little 'o' over the string, like this:

Here, the open string is perfectly good for the chord, so you should strike it with the plectrum or your fingers with no worries.

READING TAB

'Tab' is short for *tablature*, a system of writing music for the guitar that has been around for ages – at least 400 years or so, in fact. It's an alternative to reading music and, being a dedicated system, it's a lot easier to decipher. I can usually teach someone how to read tab in around 20 minutes, where any competence with reading music will take around six months or so to achieve. So you can see why it's a very popular idea and why the music books you buy in stores are generally full of it, alongside the more familiar-looking *standard notation*, which is what the generally used system of musical runes is called.

In the main, most of the music examples in this book are in both tab and standard notation, mainly because this is the way you'll find guitar music presented out there in the field and not because I'm trying to teach you how to read music. So, as far as tab is concerned, the basic grid looks like this:

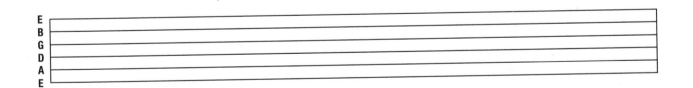

Six horizontal lines, which once again represent the guitar's strings with the bass E at the bottom. If I wanted you to play each of your open strings from bass to treble (that's bottom to top), I would simply put an 'o' on each of the strings, like this:

Acoustic Guitar

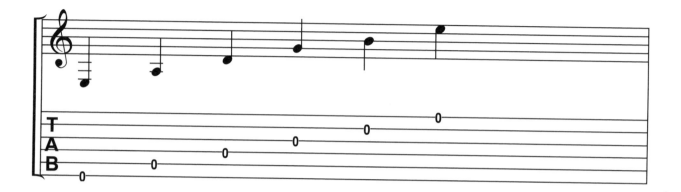

You read it from left to right, just like you're reading this sentence now. Easy, isn't it?

Of course, we can't stay on the open strings for ever, and so we have to bring in some more numbers, one for each fret, like this:

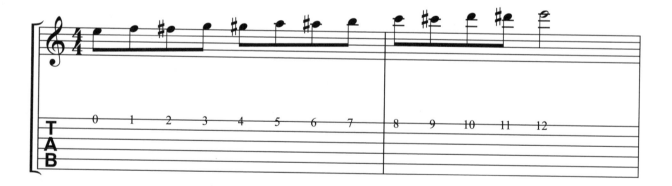

In the diagram above, the numbers on the top string are telling you to play the note found on each of the respective frets. You begin with the open string – 'o' – and then play the first fret, second, third and so on. Once again, I don't expect you to rattle this off like a pro and whizz up the neck; in fact, it's probably better that you just look at it for now and try to work out where everything fits like you did with the chord boxes a few pages ago. There will be time for working with tab once you hit the lessons themselves.

FRETBOARD DIAGRAMS

Let me introduce you to a very close cousin to the chord box, the fretboard diagram. This is really a kind of cross between tablature and the chord-box diagrams in that it tends to demonstrate some kind of movement on the fretboard as an overall shape. Guitarists love shapes, and sometimes that's a good thing and sometimes it isn't. In any case, take a look at the fretboard diagram below:

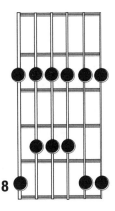

I could have written this out in tablature...

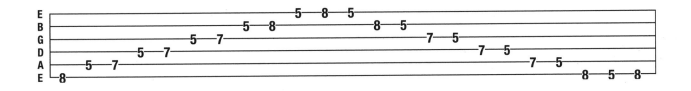

...but I think that the first diagram gives you a more immediate idea of what's going on (which is why I sometimes give you both, just as a failsafe).

You'll see quite a few fretboard diagrams in the book, but you can be sure that I've tried my hardest to give you a clear written description of what I want you to do on each occasion.

Acoustic Guitar

In this chapter, I hope to cover the kind of information that you don't even know you need yet, so feel free to give it a miss the first time around and get on with the exercises. But I'm betting that your curiosity is going to get the better of you sooner than you think...

BUYING AN ACOUSTIC GUITAR

I realise that you've probably already bought an acoustic guitar, otherwise you wouldn't be reading this book. But, like I said, this information will come in useful later on if you decide to trade up, or you might like to read through it as a kind of checklist for the instrument you've already bought.

PURE ACOUSTIC OR ELECTRO-ACOUSTIC?

I'd be the first to admit that it's a confusing old world out there – you can't even go into a coffee shop these days without making a whole series of decisions: latte, grande latte, mocha, frappe? Luckily, as far as acoustic guitars are concerned, your main choice is between two essential types: acoustic and electro-acoustic.

This distinction has little or nothing to do with the overall shape of the instrument itself – or, in very many cases, the way it looks. There are usually no cosmetic differences between the ordinary acoustic and the pickup-loaded variety until you take a good look close up. So you'll find that acoustics come in a series of preset sizes, like jumbos (big bodies), dreadnoughts (still quite big) and orchestra models (getting slightly smaller), down to parlour guitars (which really are quite small). Along the way, you might run across guitars described as *folk-sized*, and so on, but actual body size will be quite an easy choice to make: you might not want a whopping great jumbo-sized guitar, fancying instead something far more petite – it's down to taste, particularly in the early stages.

Of course, it would be such a simple world if it just meant that the bigger the body, the louder the guitar, but this isn't always the case, either. Some small-bodied guitars come with huge voices, and vice versa. This is down to the

intricacies of construction and quality of wood and not really much to do with physical dimensions.

So actually selecting your guitar from the shop window won't be too much of a nightmare – but it might be important to stop and think about whether you want to be able to plug it into an amplifier or not. One of the main reasons for this is that actually fitting a pickup system to an acoustic guitar is a job for an expert and certainly not in the realm of Mr Do-It-Yourself, however handy you might be with a Black & Decker Workmate and a set of chisels. It's far from impossible, of course, but the kind of surgery involved in retrofitting (as we guitar pundits call it) is definitely not for the squeamish.

So, what are the points for and against a guitar with onboard electronics as opposed to an ordinary, 'pure' acoustic? The first thing to understand is that building an acoustic guitar is actually quite a skilled art. The higher-range models are usually handbuilt and carry the sort of price tag that goes along with any bespoke custom build. When I say 'higher range', I'm referring to models that peg in around the £4,000–£5,000 mark – and while you regain your breath, I'll add that professional orchestra players think nothing of paying twice that for their instruments. We actually have it fairly easy by comparison.

Naturally, I'm not expecting you to have made such a wallet-boggling investment in something that you've bought just to see if you can make any headway with playing music. And good for you; there are plenty of very good instruments on the market today that will serve you well all the way up to professional use. If you've chosen wisely (and, to be honest, there's not so much that can go wrong anyway), you'll be able to cover all the material in this book with ease. Well, the instrument won't hold you back, at any rate!

If you think that you might like to play your guitar on stage with a band (or solo) one day, it makes good sense to buy an electro-acoustic as a way of future-proofing your purchase. Electro-acoustics are usually built with one basic

Acoustic Guitar

compromise in mind, though, and it's good to be aware of this from the start. Building a guitar that will respond well to the onslaught of built-in electronics is one thing, but building one that will deliver the best results acoustically is a whole different ball game. In other words, you could be talking about two completely different guitars, from the point of view of construction. Because this is an 'early learner' book and definitely not a thesis on instrument construction, excuse me if I don't go into too much detail here; just accept the fact that, if you've got it at the back of your mind to join a band and play your acoustic live, it might be a good idea to be ready. If not, no worries.

GENERAL POINTS TO WATCH

One piece of very sage advice when buying your first guitar is to take someone with you who can already play a bit. After all, if you've never played one before, it's very difficult to know exactly what your potential purchase sounds like – whether it pleases you – if you can't actually play it. Sure, you could ask the guy in the shop to play it for you, but it's always best to go along with someone whose opinion you can trust (ie someone who's not actually going to benefit from the sale!). If I was going to suggest a few simple pointers, they would be these:

- Check inside the soundhole to see if there are any unsightly blobs of glue or signs of poor workmanship. If the inside of the instrument looks like something from a primary-school woodwork class, it's quite likely that it's not going to be up to scratch in other areas.

- Check to see if the strings are high above the fretboard. If it's really hard to push the strings down at around the 12th fret because they're about half an inch off the board, put the guitar back on the wall and look at another. Pay no attention to any stories you might hear from the shopkeeper about a high playing action strengthening your fingers – it's all salesman's twaddle.

- Take a good look at all the playing surfaces – the fretboard, frets and so on. If

THE BASICS

everything looks smooth and in order, from the pure point of view of 'does it look well-built in general?', with no obvious blemishes, then the chances are that everything will be OK. Remember, you've always got the right to take something back if it doesn't do what it's meant to do.

- Try to stick to a well-known brand of guitar. Independent makers are going to hate me for this but, where beginners are concerned, it's pretty much a hard-and-fast rule. If it's a make you've heard of or seen people play on stage or on TV, the chances are it will work for you. If you're not familiar with exactly what the reputable makes are, invest some time at your local newsagent and browse through a few guitar magazines. Look out for the companies with the posh-looking full-page adverts – they're usually the ones you can rely on.

WHILE YOU'RE IN THE MUSIC SHOP... (PART I)

While you're there, I would heartily advise you to buy an electronic tuner, too. These come in all shapes and sizes, and despite the fact that it means another dent in your funds, having one will save you so much time and frustration in these early stages that you'll bless the day I told you to buy it 1,000 times.

Seriously, tuning is one of the biggest obstacles a beginner has to overcome in these early stages, and the simple investment of £20–£30 ($35–$50) or so isn't too high a price to pay for all the trouble it will save you.

There are two facts worth noting here: guitars are notorious for going out of tune practically every time you pick them up, and practising on a guitar that's out of tune is like wearing the wrong glasses. Your musical ear will eventually turn out to be your best friend, but it has to be trained a little first. The best training it will ever receive is when it hears a nicely tuned instrument all the time and not something that sounds like a spin drier full of cats. Don't even think twice – buy an electronic tuner right now!

Acoustic Guitar

WHILE YOU'RE IN THE MUSIC SHOP... (PART II)

You might even consider buying a couple more things while you're there. Unless you've bought one of these package deals that comes equipped with a strap, a soft case and some plectrums, it's definitely in your interests to buy a strap, soft case and some plectrums right from Day 1. We'll talk about the value of guitar straps in a moment, and we'll also be eavesdropping on the great pick-versus-fingers debate. And surely the soft-case option speaks for itself; if you're spending a fair chunk of cash on a precision music instrument, you don't want it lying around the house completely unprotected, do you? Guitars are quite sturdy instruments, but it's amazingly easy to put a dent in one – and surprisingly painful when it happens. I once had a student who knocked a music stand over, hitting my brand new nylon-string classical guitar, and I had to tell him it didn't matter through gritted teeth.

A WORD ABOUT NYLON-STRING GUITARS

Ages ago, when I was a mere lad buying my first guitar, it was a kind of default option to buy one that had nylon strings on it. By nature and design, this was a classical guitar, made for playing classical guitar music and not built for playing Led Zeppelin covers. I hadn't a clue in those days, of course, believing that a guitar was a guitar and we'd sort out the fine details later on. What's more, it was far easier to buy a cheap nylon-string guitar than it was to buy a cheap steel-string model. In the end it became crystal clear that it was a case of horses for courses, and I now know that classical guitars are for classical guitar music while Led Zeppelin covers sound much better on the real thing: a steel-string guitar. So, if you're tempted by a classical guitar's seemingly reasonable – nay, seductive – price tag, please think twice.

GUITAR STRINGS

It would be easy to believe that there's nothing too controversial about guitar strings, too, but you'd be wrong. In order to make things simple, I've constructed a short FAQ section on the subject of strings:

Q: How do I know what to ask for in a music shop?

A: Firstly, you want a set of acoustic guitar strings – make that very plain to the guy behind the counter, because electric-guitar strings are different from the ones you need for your guitar. Once again, I'd advise you to go for a brand that bears a familiar name. Don't buy cheap ones – you get pretty much what you pay for, and cheap strings stretch (ie go out of tune) and can sound really nasty, too.

Q: How do I know which gauge to buy?

A: Until you've racked up some experience, it's best to go for light to medium gauge. This will mean that your top string should measure in at about .010–.011 (guitar string gauges are measured in hundredths of an inch – steadfastly non-metric, us guitarists). Anything fatter than this might shred your fingertips and make playing quite a painful experience until those digits have hardened up. It's a man's life in the Royal Marines…

Q: How often do I change them?

A: Believe it or not, this can be down to body chemistry and vary enormously from one person to the next. In general, strings wear out in two ways. One is through corrosion – they're constantly coming into contact with sweaty fingers which leave all sorts of unmentionable deposits on them, which in turn kick off the process of deterioration nicely (I would go into more detail here, but some of you might just be of a sensitive disposition).

The other way a string dies is through use. It's quite a violent life for a guitar string; you get bashed against the metal frets day after day, you get bent out of shape and generally pushed and pulled about, and eventually something's got to give.

Acoustic Guitar

The giveaway signs that you need to change your strings are:

1 There's enough dirt clinging to them to start a small vegetable plot

or

2 That attractive gold colour (actually bronze) has worn off the lower four strings almost completely and turned a very unattractive black.

Both mean that a string change is long overdue.

Q: Is a string change something I can do myself?

A: Of course, but I would suggest that you get someone to show you how it's done the first couple of times. It's not rocket science, but trial and error here can be very frustrating. I once had a pupil turn up for his lesson with his electric guitar in two separate carrier bags because a string change had gone epically wrong.

WHILE YOU'RE IN THE MUSIC SHOP… (PART III)

While I'm on the subject of string changes, I'll take just a moment or two more of your time to tell you about one of the greatest inventions for guitar-playing mankind: the string winder. This marvellous little appliance fits over the tuning pegs of your guitar and allows you to wind and unwind strings about ten times faster than you would using the normal wrist 'n' twist approach. They are a little like the spanners you'd use to tighten and undo the wheel nuts on a car, and they can speed up string changing immensely. The real pros use battery-powered models, but it's easy enough to make do with one of the mechanical variety. They cost only a little, and once again you'll eventually wonder how you ever got along without one.

Acoustic Guitar

SORE FINGERS – THE TIP OF THE ICEBERG

Most players who are new to the guitar realise early on that their fingers are getting sore. Depending on how much you practise and play, this condition can range from being slightly uncomfortable to manifesting itself as blisters, torn skin and the feeling that maybe you should have chosen to play the flute instead.

We've all been there at one time or another, and we've all survived. It's merely a question of playing until your fingertips have hardened up enough to deal with all the rigours that guitar-playing life can throw at them. It can take anything from six weeks to six months for this to happen, but it always does in the end, and when it does you'll wonder what all the fuss was about.

But this bodily adaptation to playing the guitar is really only a very small part of rather a large equation. Think about it: you're asking your right and left hands and arms to do something completely new, and the chances are (if you're right handed) that your left hand has carried out only very light duties so far – and the little finger on your left hand has probably done nothing since the day you were born, apart from poke out decorously while you were drinking tea!

So there's a lot that has to happen – muscles have to develop and so on – and this takes time, so when you're walking around the house blowing on your poor, sore fingertips, just remember all the other changes that are going on under the surface. There will be things you try to do that appear to be impossible at first – your body just won't co-operate at all – but it's a question of not allowing yourself to become impatient; allow the development to happen by keeping up a daily practice schedule.

This is a topic we'll be returning to many times over the course of this book, so I won't harp on about it too much here. You'll learn the importance of doing everything in the right order – literally learning to walk before you can run – and allowing your hands slowly to become the athletes they have to be!

Acoustic Guitar

PLECTRUMS, FLESH AND FINGERPICKS

Another choice that players new to the guitar have to make fairly early on is how they plan to sound the strings with their right hands. You'll have probably seen players on TV using pieces of plastic called *plectrums*, and you'll have doubtless seen a few players playing with their fingertips, too. So which is best for you?

Well, this is something else that will be revealed in time. As he or she gains experience, each new player finds him or herself drawn more to one set of preferences in terms of choice of instrument, string gauge and type, pickup system and so on, and this will eventually turn into part of that player's overall style. Every choice we make as players counts towards the overall sound we produce, in some small way, and this is one of the reasons why there are so many diverse-sounding players out there – they've all selected the same form of instrument, but they've developed slightly different mannerisms and playing habits which add up to highly individual playing styles.

So the first thing I'd advise you to do is give everything a try, to begin with. You'll soon find out which method you prefer. In fact, it's a good idea to review everything you do on the guitar every six months or so – go back to basics and take a good look at all the various individual parts that go towards your playing technique. People change, and something that you were only too ready to dismiss six months ago might be the one thing that will get you out of a rut today.

PLECTRUMS

These little pieces of plastic, nylon or whatever come in all shapes and sizes and probably represent the cheapest piece of guitar-playing kit you'll ever buy. You can quite often pick up about six plectrums for £1 or so, and so it's worth splashing out a little and seeing which type, shape and texture takes your fancy. Regardless of shape and actual material, the most important thing you'll have to know about plectrums in these early days is that they come in a variety of different thicknesses, and the thickness you choose can have the biggest influence over the way you strike the strings, so listen up.

A very thin plectrum – say, one that weighs in at .44mm – is probably only good for strumming chords. It will be a very thin, flexible affair that bends noticeably as you strike the strings and gives a very specific dragging sound to playing chords (there's an example on the CD – Track 2). Some people love this sound, while others hate it. Once again, your choice of plectrum is one of those preferences that form the foundation of your style, and it's possibly a more important decision than you'd otherwise think.

A plectrum that weighs about .78mm is of a more medium weight and will put up a bit of a fight as it's dragged across the strings. It's a lot less flexible, and this has an effect of the sound.

Plectrums that are thicker than 1mm are known in the trade as 'man's plectrums' in some quarters because they offer absolutely no resistance to the strings and are at their best when playing the flurries of notes you hear from the guitar high-wire acts. In other words, they suit rock styles quite well, as the definition they offer for playing individual notes is at a premium.

Believe it or not, we can go even further up in terms of thickness; 2mm or even 3mm plectrums are not unheard of, but these are usually defined as being 'jazz plectrums' because not only are jazz players real men but they also use enormously thick strings – they are the real Marine commandos of picking. Not, of course, that I'm in any small way biased! (Oh, and before anyone out there points out that there are some rock players who can pick more notes per nanosecond than it's possible to count, jazz players don't use distortion on their amps to make the job of picking easier. Be afraid.)

FINGERS

Fingers come in all shapes and sizes, too, the main difference being that you can't go down to the music store and buy a thicker or thinner set to experiment with. One thing that has to be made immediately clear is that soft flesh – or even softish fingernail – is going to sound different to plastic when it comes into contact with the

Acoustic Guitar

string. Once again, something that can have an overwhelming influence on your sound as a player is really something incredibly fundamental. People often ask me if finger shape or size makes any real difference to playing, and I can honestly say that I've never known it to have much of an influence. I've known some great players to have short, stubby fingers and similarly uncommonly good ones with long, slender digits. Talent, you see, doesn't reside in the fingers, but it does in general drive us to make the best possible use of the physical attributes we're given.

You might be surprised to know that I've seen many players – particularly the ladies – give up because they didn't want to cut their left-hand fingernails. Sorry, girls, but it's true. Guitarists have notoriously short fingernails on the left hand and slightly longer ones on the right (if they play fingerstyle – more on that in a moment), and if this doesn't suit an individual's taste or sense of fashion, unfortunately there's nothing to be done. You can't play guitar with long left-hand fingernails – fact. Thankfully, there's a whole range of false fingernails available to the fashion-conscious guitarist these days, so it needn't mean the end of your brief affair with playing the guitar.

But it's the right-hand fingers we're considering at the moment, so back to the plot. There are many schools of thought that say that playing with your fingers – that is, *fingerstyle* – is the only true way of approaching the acoustic guitar, and in fact they do have quite a strong case. Think about it: instead of a single blade of plastic, you've got four independent means of sounding the strings (that's a thumb and three fingers – we don't use the right-hand little finger too much), and so a guitar sound produced by your fingers can be far more involved than it would be from a single stroke.

So fingers can give your acoustic playing a three-dimensional edge, if appropriately honed, and I wholeheartedly recommend that you try playing a little fingerstyle from Day 1. Certainly, this book encourages some early development of the fingers, as well as general plectrum-bound strumming, to give you every possible chance to add both strings to your bow, as it were.

FINGERPICKS

Of course, with every seeming dilemma comes compromise, and as far as picking is concerned, fingerpicks would seem to be exactly this. Fingerpicks are little plastic items that fit on your fingertips and thumb to give you the best of both worlds, providing you with all the dexterity usually associated with fingerstyle along with the clarity and decisiveness that you only get with hard plastic.

Of course, there's a catch: it's really not as simple as all that, and players who use finger or thumb picks form something of a minority. I can't begin to tell you why this is so, other than by putting it down to the period of adjustment involved with using fingerpicks and the fact that – as I don't believe too many players actually start off their playing lives using them – it seems like too much trouble to go back to the nursery slopes for a while in order to accommodate the change. Other than that, of course, fingerpicks are useful to you only once your general fingerstyle skills are in place. My advice here is to remember that fingerpicks are an option for later on, if you're interested in playing fingerstyle but want to increase the dynamics of your right-hand approach.

SONG BOOKS

In an ideal world, it would be possible to go into a music store, find some music you wanted to play written out in book form, buy it and go home and play it. This simple ambition formed pretty much a consensus amongst my pupils; few of them had their eyes upon playing Wembley Arena, but most wanted to attain the degree of skill necessary to pick and choose from music's mainstream at will. You'd be forgiven for thinking that this must surely be an easy wish to grant, but unfortunately it's not. I don't want to cast a shadow across your guitar-playing ideals this early on in your career, but there are a few things about the real world that I feel obliged to draw your attention towards.

About 30 years ago, it was practically impossible to buy a music book that even remotely resembled the music it was meant to contain. I saw some pretty far-fetched things come into my teaching room in those days, including the classic

Acoustic Guitar

AC/DC portfolio that was, in fact, written for piano! It was commonplace to find that the books contained the wrong chords, and basically everything was in a complete mess. In fact, I think the first thing I ever had published in *Guitarist* magazine was a letter bemoaning the fact that the music book that went along with one of the biggest-selling albums of the '80s was laughably inaccurate and how it was driving me, a teacher, nuts.

Things improved once the music publishers of the world began to realise that guitarists wanted to play the guitar parts from their favourite albums and songs and not a dreadful hash-up put together by an impoverished music student who was earning himself some extra pizza-and-beer money on the side. They began to take things a lot more seriously, and it became increasingly accepted that you'd get a fair reading of any particular song – guitar chords, riffs and solos – from most of the books you bought.

I've still got a lot of reservations about 'playing by numbers', and I often challenge my students at seminars by asking why, if they've got access to transcriptions of the songs they want to learn either from music shops or even the internet, they're sitting there looking at me? After a lot of uncomfortable shuffling around, they realise that I'm joking and we remain friends – but there is a very serious point underlying the challenge, none the less.

So, in short, buy music books by all means – with a bit of practice, some intuition and a little informed guesswork, you'll end up with a good-to-great reading of the song you want to learn – but be selective. You'll learn what to look out for soon enough, but there might be a few disappointments in the pipeline initially.

POSTURE

Most instruments come with an accepted playing posture. If you were learning piano, you'd expect to learn sitting on a stool and you'd be told to keep your fingers straight over the keyboard, things like that. If you were learning cello,

you'd be told to keep your back straight and stick the instrument between your knees. So it would go for most other instruments you could name. But the guitar has rather a rogue nature, in that one single posture has never really had the chance to emerge into the light of general acceptability. Sure, classical players will tell you that posture is incredibly important and as rigid as a straitjacket (take a look at any classical player in a performance and you'll see what I mean), while it would also appear that, with steel-strung acoustic guitar, anything goes.

Think about this for a few moments. Why is it that instrument teachers apply a certain amount of dogma to the simple act of sitting down and addressing your chosen instrument? The answer, in general, is that any acceptable playing position you care to mention has been worked out and modified over the years, until the version which allows optimum levels of performance has been achieved. In other words, by adopting the tried-and-tested playing positions, you're allowing yourself the best possible access to your instrument – and that means it's going to make playing the darned thing as easy as possible.

As I've said, no such rigid principles have been applied to playing steel-string guitar – and that includes electric guitar, too. Take a good, long look at all the players you can find and the best you could say is that there is obviously some kind of common denominator at work, but nothing too formal. After all, rock 'n' roll is hardly formal, is it? This is pretty much the set of rules we apply to everything we, as guitarists, do: if it's not classical, it's got at least a whiff of rock 'n' roll about it.

So how do we go about making sure that posture serves the joint masters of general accessibility and looking acceptably cool at the same time? It all depends on a couple of pieces of metal...

Take a look at the very bottom end of your guitar – that's the bit on the outer rim of the instrument, in line with the strings – and see if there's a metal plug there. If there is, it's what's known as a *strap peg*, and somewhat surprisingly these

Acoustic Guitar

don't necessarily travel in pairs. It's fairly commonplace to have one at the end of the instrument, but it's rarer to find another one around the base of the neck. Obviously you need two if you're going to fit a guitar strap successfully, so it comes as a bit of a shock sometimes to find only one.

The reason for this singularity is down to traditions in manufacture that stretch back into the mists of guitar-making time. Once upon a time, you see, it was uncommon for players to stand up to play, and so the matter of attaching a strap didn't really come into the equation. When it did – in a manner that probably became made most popular during the rock 'n' roll-drenched 1950s – manufacturers started to attach strap pegs, but only at one end. The idea was that you actually tied the strap to your headstock with a sort of shoelace affair. And so today, this tradition is still honoured in quite a few areas, although it's almost unknown to tie the strap on anymore.

So, if your guitar has a strap peg on the body end of the guitar and another one somewhere at the base of the neck, all's well and I would invite you to read the paragraphs below about buying a guitar strap. If not, all is not lost, but you might want to consider having another fitted – by someone who knows what they're doing; let's avoid any DIY for now – at a later date.

Posture is an important consideration in that it ensures you the optimum opportunity to learn the ropes the correct way, and one of the easiest ways of doing this is by attaching a strap to your guitar, even if you play sitting down. Ideally, you should adjust it so that your guitar is in the same playing position when you're sitting down as it is when you're standing up. I've seen a great number of students who've learnt something sitting down then find that they can't play it on stage because their posture has changed.

Other than that, the golden rules are: keep your back straight, relax your arms, keep your wrists as straight as possible and try not to practise while you're slumped in front of the television (we all do it, and we all know it's wrong).

GUITAR STRAPS

Another accessory that comes in all shapes and sizes, the guitar strap is quite a common-sense affair. Obviously colour and material aren't going to make an enormous amount of difference to your playing, but, as with everything, there are a few guidelines it's probably worth noting.

The first concerns colour. I made the mistake of buying a really ornate guitar strap when I bought my first guitar. In fact, I think the shop threw it in – probably the only way they could get rid of the thing; there can't be too many teenage boys who would buy a guitar strap covered in red roses, after all... As it was, I was blinded by the excitement of buying my first electric guitar, and I would have accepted anything that came for free! Of course, I went out and bought myself something altogether more manly and 'rock' later on and have since found that the fashion-world maxim 'black goes with anything' applies to guitar straps, too. Literally, I own only three or four guitar straps, they're all black and they all go with every guitar I've got (currently about 17). But don't let me put you off if you've set your heart on something in lime green...

The important point to realise is that two things are paramount. Quality of workmanship counts for everything here, and it shows up particularly around the leather or plastic 'thongs' that actually do the job of attaching your guitar. I've seen some unbelievably shoddy-looking straps in my time with lightweight attachments that you just know are going to wear through in an instant and possibly tear or break, and nobody likes the idea of your precious instrument hitting the deck owing to a poorly made strap, so make sure that yours looks tough enough to withstand the push and pull of everyday guitar life. If it's actually quite difficult to get your strap peg through the hole in the strap, so much the better; it means it's not going to come off too easily, either.

The other important factor, again often overlooked, concerns the width and level of adjustability present in the guitar strap. Width is important because it spreads the weight of the guitar evenly over your shoulder (it might not feel heavy now,

Acoustic Guitar

but even the lightest guitar can exert a drag on your shoulder after a while), so in many ways, the thicker the better. What I'm really saying is that you should try to avoid straps that are only an inch or so wide. Anything above that should do the job pretty well.

Level of adjustability, meanwhile, should speak for itself. Just like with a car's seat belts (guitar straps are often made from a similar material, in fact), you want to be able to adjust your strap for comfort, and so the more adjustments you can make, the better. Make sure that it's easy to adjust the length of the strap without having to call upon any heavy hydraulic gear. Meanwhile, another frill you might like to invest in is a bit of padding at the point where the strap goes over your shoulder – not absolutely necessary, but a nice (if somewhat deluxe) touch.

As to how high you should wear your guitar, it's a question of common sense. I've interviewed many players who wear their guitars really low, and they've all admitted that the only reason they do so is to look cool. The fact is that too low or too high is impractical, because it means that you have to 'reach' for the instrument and distort yourself accordingly. This is universally a bad thing, as it introduces a guitarist's worst enemy – tension – into your body. Tension slows you down and inhibits freedom of movement, so try to eliminate it at all times.

To calculate the optimum height for your guitar, try this simple test. Stand up with both arms hung at your side. Now bend your left arm at the middle until it's slightly lower than your shoulder. If there's no tension in your arm and you feel relaxed in this position, this is the height to adjust your strap to so that the guitar neck fits into your left hand at this point. This calibration will take a bit of trial and error, but it's quite an important thing to get right in the early days.

PRACTICE TIME: YOUR WORKBENCH

Of all the frequently asked questions, 'How long should I practise?' is arguably the most common. It's also one of the hardest to answer, mainly because of our negative attitudes towards practising in general. It might have something to do

38

with the music lessons we had at school when we were children, I don't know, but the immediate association we tend to make with practice is that it's boring, tedious, repetitive and dull. So, when people ask me THE QUESTION, the answer they're really looking for is along the lines of, 'Oh, you don't need to practise at all. Everything will fall into place naturally, you'll see.' And I really wish that was the answer I could give people, sometimes, because I feel such a hard-hearted disciplinarian when I tell them the truth.

What I try to do is explain to people exactly what should be happening when they practise and attempt to turn this negative image into a positive one. The way I see it, when you learn a musical instrument – any instrument – you're really addressing two things: one is learning music itself and the other is acquiring the technique necessary to make the instrument work. These two things, music and technique, must be in perfect balance at all times if you're to progress as an instrumentalist.

As an example, I can obviously read music, and I know an awful lot about theory, and so on – of course I do; it's my job. But I also know where all the notes are on a piano, and yet I still can't play it. Why? Well, my knowledge of music is fine, but I've got practically no piano technique at all. In other words, the sheer basement fact that I don't know how to make that particular music machine work with any real flow is the only thing holding me back. I can't play a flute because I don't know where any of the notes are, so I'm well and truly screwed in that area, too. But as far as the guitar is concerned, my knowledge of music and my technical ability is in an almost Zen-like balance, and so one is free to serve the other.

Another way of looking at it is to say that the act of writing this book is a combination of learning to operate a machine – a word processor, typewriter (remember those?) or pen – and having something to write with it. If you can type at an impressive 150 words a minute, it's meaningless unless you've actually got something to write. In that situation, your technical ability would be seriously out of balance with your finesse with the language.

Acoustic Guitar

So guitar practice has got to address both of these areas simultaneously in order to ensure that your development is both as fast and as balanced as possible. This is something I was very much aware of when I designed the various lessons in the rest of this book – that you're engaged in a balancing act between gaining fluency in musical exercises whilst similarly gaining technical skills at the same time.

So what's all this got to do with practice? How can we visualise this in a positive way and stop looking it as a 'necessary evil'? Well, it's mainly a question of adjusting your mindset to the extent that you begin to see your practice time as your workbench – somewhere that construction or maintenance is taking place.

Picture a man who build models out of matchsticks. He might turn out some impressive work – battleships, cathedrals and so on – all made from these tiny component parts. He might only find enough time to work on his creations for 20 minutes a night, but he's working towards a positive goal: completing his model.

Now we can all take a few steps back and agree that what's happening here is essentially a creative process, even though a lot of it is repetitive (matchsticks and glue, matchsticks and glue, etc). He's not fixing something that's broken; he's not righting wrongs; he's working towards a very positive objective. Similarly, if you start off thinking that your practice time is like a workbench and that you're building something in small, incremental steps that you will eventually be proud of, you'll be on your way to thinking of this time in a more beneficial and positive manner.

Of course, I still haven't answered the question yet, have I? OK, my take on how long somebody should practise is simply this: little and often is better than once a week. I realise that we live in a very hectic world – homework, domestic chores and busy, time-invasive work schedules drain away our free time to the extent that sometimes spending time on our hobbies is practically impossible – but ten minutes a day shouldn't be beyond any of us, and this kind of consistency is all that's needed to ensure that your playing develops. Sure, development is going to be slow, but in most cases, what's the hurry?

When I was involved pretty much exclusively with private one-on-one tuition, I could always tell if a student hadn't practised during the week or tried to squeeze everything in an hour just before his lesson, so I became quite a devout believer in the 'little and often' rule to aiding general progress on the guitar.

AVOIDING RSI

In terms of word association, when I hear the title *Crash Course* I begin to hear sirens and see flashing blue lights. You might think that no one can possibly get hurt with such a seemingly innocuous pastime as learning the guitar, and it's true that we've got a lower casualty rate than many other activities associated with free time. Even something like learning to ride a bike is renowned for causing the occasional grazed knee, but guitar playing? What could possibly go wrong?

Well, in truth, the answer is not an awful lot, but there is the very slight danger of something called RSI (Repetitive Strain Injury). Now, this isn't something that's uniquely linked to playing the guitar, or any instrument for that matter. You can get RSI from sitting poorly at a word processor writing books (although I've been lucky so far) or from operating any machine in a semi-continuous, mechanical fashion. What RSI adds up to, in simple terms, is undue wear and tear on the body's internal bits and pieces (tendons and so on) through asking them to do things for which they weren't designed in an inopportune way (most cases of RSI are down to poor posture). And playing the guitar certainly comes under that category.

Take a look at the most basic playing position while you're holding a guitar. Your left hand can easily become curled up unnaturally while you're trying to finger those awkward chords, and your picking hand might not fare any better. We're asking the hands and arms to do things that fall well outside the original blueprints for the human body, and despite the fact that it's usually very adaptable under most circumstances, there are some guidelines to observe if you want to stay out of the doctor's surgery.

Acoustic Guitar

Most of the advice you need to observe on how to avoid RSI is common sense. Any sign of pain or discomfort on the hands, arms, wrists or whatever and you do two things immediately:

1 Put down the guitar and take a break;

2 Look at your playing position and see if any modifications are necessary.

As I've said already – and it really doesn't matter how many times you hear it – tension is your worst enemy, and so if you've been sitting with your back bent in a huddle over the guitar fretboard, it's possible that you've been inviting trouble. Backs like to be straight; it keeps them healthy. Wrists and arms need the occasional look, too, and you'd be advised to keep the wrists as straight as possible and keep a check on any part of your arm or shoulder that might be experiencing undue strain. Learn to relax while you play and you'll stay out of trouble. Many players have told me that certain players they've seen in concert make everything look so easy, but this is mostly because the artists in question have learnt that all-important lesson of ridding their playing of tension.

NO PAIN, NO GAIN

Having said all that, of course, remember when we were talking about sore fingers and I said that there were muscles and so on that had to be developed in order for you to take on the hurdle race that is learning guitar? Well, to put it another way, you can expect to feel some sensation in your arms, wrists, fingers, etc, while these things happen, but there's a huge difference between positive, muscle-developing sensation and negative, risky pain.

Imagine that during every practice session your hands are working out in a gym. The sensations you're experiencing ought to feel like the development inside is positive and beneficial – just like that warm glow you get after some physical exercise. So warm glows are fine; continuous aches, pins and needles or loss of sensation are not.

RIGHT OR LEFT HANDED?

It might be too late for me to say this, but if you're one of the left-handed people in the world and you've searched high and low for a shop that stocks left-handed guitars, it's just possible that you've got things – literally – the wrong way around. I don't know where the idea of a left-handed guitar came from originally – after all, there isn't a left-handed piano or a left-handed flute, and concert violinists learn to play right-handed irrespective of which hand they use to write. So what's it all about?

In actual fact, I'm told that there are degrees of left- and right-handedness and that it's actually quite rare to find someone who is 100% either way. It's more likely that you're biased one way or the other to a certain degree, which shows up in the way you deploy your hands. As an example, I write with my right hand (although technically I use both hands, because the majority of my writing is at a computer keyboard) but I do an awful lot of other stuff with my left. What's more, there are many left-handed people out there who happen to be very adept guitarists but who have opted to play in a right-handed configuration. These people include Mark Knopfler, Gary Moore, Robert Fripp and Joe Pass, to name but a few – all celebrated for being top players in their own particular fields.

When you think about it, left- or right-handedness means that one of your hands enjoys a higher degree of dexterity than the other, and in this way left-handed people actually have an advantage over us right handers. On the guitar, an awful lot of the tricky work is carried out by the left hand; this is the hand that's in charge of the fretboard, and as we'll see it can have a great influence over the sound you're making, from a tonal point of view.

On a right-handed player, it can take ages to 'wake up' the left hand and literally bring it up to a baseline level of efficiency in order to carry out all its duties. Meanwhile, of course, the right hand – super-efficient through years of experience with pens, scissors and can openers – has a comparatively easy life strumming chords! In fact, I've found that left-handed players tend to

Acoustic Guitar

advance faster than right handers if they play the guitar in a right-handed configuration.

If you've bought a left-handed guitar based on the fact that you do everything else this way around, and so why not?, I would advise you at least to try playing the other way around, even if it means borrowing another guitar for a couple of weeks. You might otherwise be turning your back on one of the very few physical advantages you can bring to the instrument.

DON'T BELIEVE EVERYTHING YOU HEAR

Now, I know that I'm in danger of sounding like a cynical old man at this point, but I want to say a few words about an important aspect of learning music that I believe to have been all but suffocated in these modern times.

When I was learning guitar, my friends and I would buy records, listen to them and try to imitate not only the notes we heard but also the way in which those notes were being played. We got an awful lot of our tonal information from merely listening, and through trial and error with guitars in hand we generally found that we were able to come up with something passably close after a little bit of work.

Back in the 1970s, what you saw was pretty much what you got. If you knew that a player was playing a Gibson Les Paul guitar through a Marshall amp, then armed with the same or very similar equipment yourself (and some considerable effort) you could get tonally in the same ball park. In those days, studio trickery and special effects were in their infancy – and having a computer in your living room or bedroom was still something that happened only in science-fiction films.

Today, we take special effects in movies for granted. We all know how it's done – especially if we plough through all the 'making of' information on the DVD when it hits the shops. But I'm constantly surprised when I meet people who don't think that technology has yet reached the recording studio. Of course it has, and

today it's a case of sometimes what you think is happening is actually the result of some clever programming and not necessarily raw talent.

For instance, in pop circles it's depressingly common to find 'live' bands actually miming on stage – and not just when they're doing TV shows, either. If they're not miming 100%, you can bet that some of the backing vocals are stored on disc somewhere hidden from view. I know of quite a few bands for certain who use backing tracks – recorded in the studio and mimed to live – when they perform. There's even a machine in the studio that will help teenage girl/boy bands sing in tune, believe it or not!

So what's all this got to do with the job of learning to play acoustic guitar? All I'm saying is that, if you hear a guitar sound on a CD, the chances are it was put through heaven knows what kind of equipment after it left the instrument in the studio and before it turned up on that shiny little disc. In fact, with recent advances in studio technology, it might not even be a guitar you're listening to...

Obviously I can get very grumpy about this, as my whole life's work has been about making everything that leaves my fingers on the guitar sound right, and yet the same (some would say better) results are now obtainable out of a box. All I'm asking from you is a healthy amount of cynicism when you listen to a CD or see a band. And finally, just to confirm that I really am a gold-card-carrying member of the Grumpy Old Man Squad, it's my belief that you can't win fame on a TV game show!

DO YOU HAVE TO LEARN TO READ MUSIC?

This is another one of those questions that's quite high on the agenda for someone starting out on an instrument. The answer varies between instruments – and sometimes between styles of music on a single instrument, for that matter. For instance, if you were about to embark on learning to play classical guitar, then I'm afraid that reading music is mandatory. The whole discipline involved with learning the classical variant of our instrument is tied inextricably to reading music from the page. The same is true for practically all orchestral instruments,

Acoustic Guitar

and it would be a wise course to take for anyone who has their sights set on a career in music as an instrumentalist. It's the native language, after all.

As far as steel-strung acoustic or electric guitar are concerned, reading music isn't mandatory, mainly because there isn't really a written music tradition associated with those instruments. With classical guitar, virtually everything you learn has been written down, but with modern rock or pop guitar there's still a very healthy aural tradition – many people still learn by playing along to records.

So my answer in full would be this: If you want to go into music – in any sense of the word – professionally, learning to read would make some kind of sense. If, however, you're looking to play for a hobby, or even semi-professionally, reading music is far from being obligatory.

HOW TO PRACTISE

We've already taken a look at practising in the previous section, but there I was more concerned with trying to answer the question 'How long should I practise?' than simply '*How* should I practise?'. If you're saying to yourself, 'Surely practising means just sitting down and getting on with it,' you're nearly right. Nearly...

The best and most effective practising depends largely on what kind of attitude you adopt when you approach it. For instance, just like any kind of physical exercise, it's best to try to turn practice into a habit – a once-daily ritual performed at roughly the same time every day. In this way, practising will become part of your daily routine, like brushing your teeth, and in this respect it's best if you try to do your practice at the same time each day – and I say this even though I know only too well that domestic craziness often means that this simply isn't always possible. But, as a basic plan, it's a great idea.

Another thing to consider is where to practise. I had a pupil once who used to try to practise in the living room while his family were watching TV (you can imagine how popular that made him!), and of course it simply didn't work. In order to practise efficiently, you need peace and quiet, preferably in a place away from the hustle and bustle of family life. I'm not going to suggest that you disappear off to the garden shed with your guitar every night, but if you can find a clear space amidst the turmoil of modern life, go for it.

The other thing I'm going to insist on here is that you try your best to practise on a chair and definitely not slouched in an armchair or on a sofa in front of the TV. It's absolutely vital that these early weeks of practising are spent with the best possible chance of setting you on the path for all the correct and beneficial practice habits. It's the easiest thing in the world to pick up some bad ones that will actually impede and hinder your progress, so just go and find a proper chair, all right?

Seeing as you're going to be working from this book a lot of the time while you practise, you'll need something to prop it up. The floor's no good for this (look,

Acoustic Guitar

generations have tried this, so you don't have to), and a table isn't ideal, either; you need something to keep the pages open and in plain sight, like a book stand. The best solution is probably a music stand, which you can pick up at a jumble, yard or boot sale for a few pence. They're designed for one thing only: to keep pages of music in full view of the musician. They even have clips to keep the pages open. Problem solved!

WEEK 1

Guitar playing can basically be stripped down to two essential elements: playing chords and playing individual notes. You can think of this as the difference between playing an accompaniment to a song and playing its melody, if you like. In any case, during this first week, we're going to be looking at the fundamentals of both these activities. This will include:

- Learning about tuning;

- Playing your first chords;

- Playing your first melody notes;

- Changing chords.

DAY 1: WELCOME!

Today's goal is to learn about tuning and to play some notes.

> **QUOTE FOR THE DAY**
>
> Picks are for fairies! – *Jeff Beck*

 The first job of the day is to make sure that your guitar is in tune. To this end, an electronic tuner is an absolute boon in these early stages (and many of the later ones, too), so if you haven't got one yet, I'd recommend a field trip to the music store. The only problem with practically all other methods of tuning is that they all rely on your ear being able to tell if a string is pitched either too high (which those in the know call *sharp*) or too low (*flat*). In the early days, your ear won't be able to do this with any acceptable degree of accuracy, as it needs to be trained, so your best option is to use an electronic tuner for the time being. I'd also advise you to watch another guitarist tuning, too, as this will give you some idea of the movements necessary to get a guitar in tune.

We'll look at a way that you can check your tuning by ear later on, but for now, if you're quite sure that your tuning is as good as it can be, let's get on with something practical.

PRACTICAL EXERCISE

For all practical exercises, make sure that you're sitting down and holding the guitar naturally. A straight-backed chair is best. Balance the guitar on your knee, preferably with a strap to support it properly and to make sure you don't drop it. It takes a while before you start to feel comfortable or natural with a guitar, and so a strap is a perfect precaution that will prevent most accidents.

Acoustic Guitar

EXAMPLES

Today, we're going to play some open strings. This will get your right hand working and give you a chance to read some tablature without too much effort. If you have to watch what's going on with your right and left hands as well as read tab, it's a little like a three-ring circus: you're never really quite sure where to look first! It doesn't really matter what you use to sound the strings here – use a plectrum if you've got one, or your thumb if you haven't; we'll refine both plectrum and fingerstyle techniques as we go along. Your main priority is to sound some notes.

Look at the tab above. All those 'o' symbols are telling you that you're supposed to sound the open strings of the guitar, one at a time. (Look back to the section on reading tab if you're unsure about what's going on.) Try to make each of the notes the same volume, using downstrokes with either your plectrum or thumb.

Acoustic Guitar

The previous diagram is a variation on the previous exercise – it's all the same notes, but they're in a different order.

The open strings on the guitar are tuned E A D G B E from bottom to top. As you play the exercises, try to say the names of the strings as you do so – it will help you with your basic orienteering.

DAY 2: BRINGING THE LEFT HAND INTO PLAY

As with Day 1, your first task of the day (and every day) is to make sure your guitar is in tune. Remember, playing on an out-of-tune guitar is like wearing badly adjusted spectacles!

Today, the left hand is going to see some action. We're going to attempt to play a couple of fretted notes and have them come out clean. Before we start, though, there are a couple of things you need to know about the left hand.

The most important thing about left-hand position for playing guitar is your thumb, which should do the job of supporting your fingers – literally giving them something to press against – as well as the more rudimentary task of holding the neck. Here's a picture of a good left-hand thumb position:

Notice how the thumb is upright and not leaning over towards the left or right. This is essential for providing proper support for the fingers

Acoustic Guitar

Note that here the thumb is upright – just like you were giving someone the 'thumbs up' sign – and not leaning to either the left or right. Many early learners lay the thumb down in line with the guitar neck, and this hampers progress. With your thumb in this position, it supports the fingers properly.

PRACTICAL EXERCISE

Before you begin today's practical work, once again make sure that you're sitting properly. Remember that you're forming playing habits that will last your playing lifetime, and it really will pay you well to set off in the right direction straight away.

EXAMPLES

This exercise calls for you to place your first finger on the third fret of the top string, as shown here:

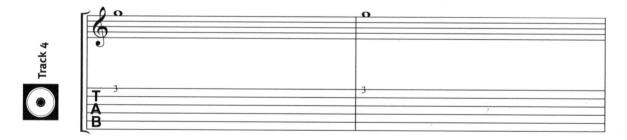

Use the tip of your first (ie index) finger – not the fleshy pad – to hold down the note. Be sure to keep the fingertip away from the string next to it as you do so, or you'll get a rather ugly buzzing sound.

Strike the note as before and listen hard. Does it sound as clear as the open string, or does it sound muted, indistinct or buzzy? If it doesn't sound quite right, adjust the position of your finger a little and check that your thumb hasn't slipped. Don't hit the string too hard, either, as this will make the string over-vibrate and sound nasty.

See the way that the finger is seated just behind the fret to ensure a good 'lock' and also how it is up on its tip and not the fleshy 'fingerprint area'

Something else to avoid is bunching the other fingers of the left hand up into a fist, as this will introduce tension into the hand and impede progress. Relax the other fingers. If it feels strange, just remind yourself that everything will feel strange for a while!

DAY 2 STUDY

Everything covered in this book is cumulative in nature. In other words, just because you've got another task to perform, that doesn't mean you can forget about yesterday's exercise altogether. So today's study is to play the open-string exercises, name the notes and then try to fret today's note with your first finger. And if you want to give the new note in your arsenal a name, it's called *G*.

Acoustic Guitar

DAY 3: YOUR FIRST CHORD

Part of learning economically (which is kind of what we're involved in here, if you hadn't already worked it out) is making the most of what you know, and this is a practice we're going to put fully into play today. On Day 2 you learned how to fret your first note, and so today you'll be using it to make your first chord. As I said at the beginning of this week, music is made up of individual notes (melody) and chords (harmony), and both are very important things to become acquainted with as soon as possible.

We're also going to learn another bit of music vocabulary: the word *arpeggio*. This is a word that literally means 'harp-like', and it's a term we ascribe to the sound of a chord being played one note at a time.

As far as the job of sounding the strings is concerned, it's time now to use your pick (which is another word for *plectrum*, if you haven't come across it before). We'll be looking at both pick and fingerstyle as we go on, in order to give you a pretty much equal grounding in both.

Do I have to mention making sure that your guitar is in tune before you do anything else? Make tuning a strict discipline and your ears will thank you for it later on, believe me.

Let's take everything we've done so far and put a new spin on it, shall we? You might want to check out the section on reading chord boxes before tackling today's little challenge...

EXAMPLES

Believe it or not, you already know a couple of different chords, so let's look at them in chord boxes:

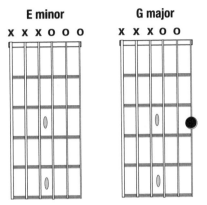

Remember that if there's a little 'x' over the string, it means that you don't play it. Just as a backup, let's look at both of these chords again in tab form:

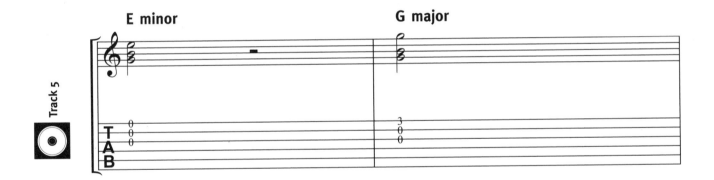

When chords are shown in tab form, the numbers relating to the frets are piled up vertically. Here, you're dealing with zeros (indicating the open strings) and the number 3, which represents the note you played in the previous lesson (which is the note G, in case you've forgotten).

PRACTICAL EXERCISE

Here's your task for today. First of all, play both your chords with a single stroke of the plectrum, taking care to avoid the strings that are marked with an 'x'. Next, play them again one string at a time, as shown in the tab below:

Acoustic Guitar

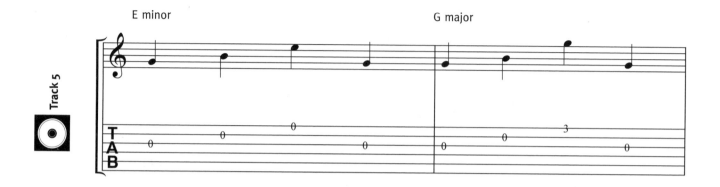

E minor　　　　　　　　　　　　　G major

Once again, make sure all the notes ring with an equal volume.

DAY 3 STUDY

As you play the chords, either as arpeggios or as musical units, say their names
out loud: 'E minor', 'G major'; it's been proved many times that saying something
out loud helps you learn it. Also, remember the exercises from the previous
couple of days; make sure you keep them idling in the background because
everything will count towards your progress.

DAY 4: MORE CHORDS AND ARPEGGIOS

As usual, the first job for today is to make sure that your guitar is in tune. I figure that if I remind you every day for a week, tuning will become a habit – it's certainly one of the better ones you can have!

So far, you've learnt two chords – in fact you might have become so proud of your achievement that you've played your entire repertoire to someone who already plays, only to be told, 'They're not real chords.' In fact, they *are* real chords; it's just that they don't yet spread across all six strings of the guitar. I say this now because I know how easy it is to become daunted in these early days, especially when someone out there offers you an entirely unsolicited critique of your achievements so far. The best advice – although I know it's hard – is to ignore it. Just press on with what you're doing. Things are set to become a whole lot more musical soon.

PRACTICAL EXERCISE

Today, I'm going to show you another two chords. Like the others, they both involve only one finger and so they won't present you with too much of a challenge.

EXAMPLES

Here's the first one:

C major

Acoustic Guitar

It's called C major. As before, try to be really careful when sounding the strings, as straying too far will make the chord sound wrong, and that won't do your ears any good at all.

The second chord is a variation of the G chord we've already looked at. Its name is G7, and once again I don't want you to worry about why chords have different names at this stage. Just take everything at face value and it will all begin to make some kind of sense in the end.

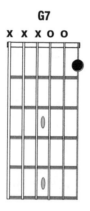

As before, we'll turn both of these new chords into arpeggios while we're at it...

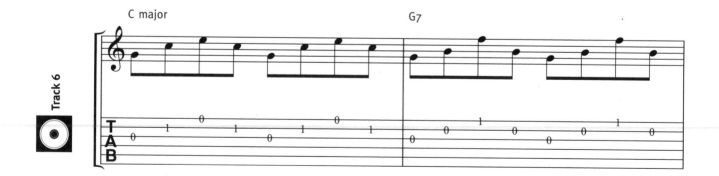

Track 6

60

Pick each string cleanly, making sure that the sound you're producing is clear and not muted or blocked by the finger fretting the note, which is a common problem and usually results in a buzzing, fuzzy sound which isn't at all pleasant. You'll be able to detect any such 'rogue' notes immediately if you play each string individually. Take your time. If you find any muted notes, make some small adjustments to your fretting finger – make sure it's standing up on its tip and not slouching over a neighbouring string.

DAY 4 STUDY

Review everything we've done so far – both in chord and arpeggiated forms – making an effort to commit the various shapes and strategies to memory as you do so. Aim for a good, clean reading of each chord, taking things slowly and patiently.

Acoustic Guitar

DAY 5: LEARNING ABOUT CHORD ARRANGEMENTS

You've reached the stage now where you know four chords, so it's time for us to have a look at a little bit of written music. Fear not, I don't mean all the strange squiggly hieroglyphics that you see in formal music; I mean the type that's going to be the most use to you right now: the notation of chord arrangements. (And I bet you thought I wasn't going to mention tuning today, but I am, so if you haven't done so already, trot off to fetch your electronic tuner or other substitute device and jump to it!)

PRACTICAL EXERCISE

When a song is written down, it's based around what's known as a *chord arrangement*, a series of chords that pins its harmony down so that it does the job of supporting the melody. Every song has a chord arrangement, even if it's only suggested somewhere along the line, and it can be anything from two or three chords to many more, although only a handful is the norm. Indeed, once upon a time it used to be said that you could play just about any song with only three chords. And actually, that's not far from the truth.

EXAMPLES

Take a look at this example:

Track 7

| Gmaj / / / |

Here we have a self-contained box (called a *bar*) which has a chord name on the left-hand side and three forward-slash symbols after it. What this means is that you're required to play the chord of G major four times: the chord symbol, or name, counts as one, with the lines counting as the other three. Try it, and listen to the example on the CD for reference, just to make sure you're playing it right.

Track 7

| Gmaj / / / | Cmaj / / / |

Now there are two bars, with a different chord at the start of each, and here you'd play the G chord four times followed by the C chord four times. And it will be about now that you hit your first real hurdle.

Changing between chord shapes is usually the first nightmarish situation encountered by guitar students. It's particularly tricky because everything is happening at once – you're checking your right and left hands to make sure that both are positioned correctly, and the chances are you're still checking out the music in the book to make sure you're changing between the correct shapes! It's a frenzy of activity, but don't worry because this kind of 'first chord-change panic' situation doesn't last for long. You'll soon be able to remember the shapes concerned and your fingers will soon learn where they're meant to be and what they're meant to be doing – and that cuts the workload down by about 75%, giving your brain the space to get on with the job of focusing on playing the music.

DAY 5 STUDY

Today's study is the most challenging yet, summoning up all chord-changing's demons. We've got to apply some military precision to the proceedings because we can't afford to ignore one of music's more important elements: timekeeping. So this exercise doesn't just call on you to change chords; you have to do so on the beat.

Track 7

| Gmaj / / / | Gmaj / / / | Gmaj / / / | Gmaj / / / |
| Cmaj / / / | Cmaj / / / | Cmaj / / / | Cmaj / / / |

The trick here is to do things dead slow. Don't rush into it so that everything comes to a grinding halt when you have to change chords, as this breaks the flow of the music and sounds really nasty. Instead, note how long it takes you to change from the G to the C and play the rest of the exercise at that precise speed – a sort of 'full-ahead slow' type of situation. If it sounds like there's a pause when you change chords, you're trying to play the exercise too fast.

Acoustic Guitar

DAY 6: MORE CHORD CHANGES!

The chances are that yesterday's practical exercise proved more demanding than you expected. Chord changes are well known for causing snags in the early days, and I fully understand how frustrating it can be when you seem to be permanently stuck in first gear in this respect. However, the good news is that we've all been there at one time or another and we've all managed to overcome the difficulties involved in just a short while, so don't be discouraged if things aren't going too well. The key to learning is the three Ps: patient, persistent practice.

PRACTICAL EXERCISE

Today, we'll take what we learned yesterday a step forward by introducing the other chords we've been looking at into our chord arrangement. Too much too soon? I don't think so. Remember, no one is expected to crack exercises like this in a single day – you can't expect to be word-perfect after a single reading. Everything looked at here goes onto that workbench called 'practice time' and can be considered a work in progress. (Oh, and you have tuned your guitar today, haven't you?)

EXAMPLE

Just so you don't get too hidebound with turning back to refresh your memory, here again are the four chords we've looked at so far:

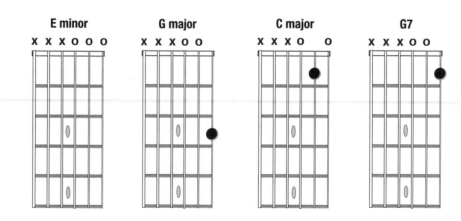

I know I asked you to try to commit them to memory a few days ago, but I think it's more comforting to know that they're right in front of you on the page when you're attempting something fairly complex. After all, it's one less thing to remember!

When songs are written, they aren't just a stream of random chords; the rules of music (which really needn't concern us for now) see to it that chords follow each other in quite predictable patterns. This is good news for you and me, because it means that we're likely to see the same chord arrangements time and time again in different songs. So, just when you thought there was no way you could possibly get good at changing between all the hundreds of different chords that abound in music, I'm telling you that there's no need even to try. It's not a mathematical thing where you have to learn to connect an infinite number of shapes together; it's a lot more predictable than that.

DAY 6 STUDY

On to today's study piece. There's every chance that you'll find that this example sounds more like a piece of actual music rather than just another task. I've certainly tried to construct it so that there's a kind of musical payoff, in any case.

Track 8

| Cmaj / / / | Cmaj / / / | Emin / / / | Emin / / / |
| Gmaj / / / | Gmaj / / / | G7 / / / | Cmaj / / / |

Study the example above and you'll see that it calls on you to use the complete chordal database that we've put together so far. The rules are as before: whatever you do, don't rush things so that you falter at every chord change. And always aim for smooth chord changes, never rushed or hesitant ones; any slip-ups due to speed come across in the music and spoil its flow.

Acoustic Guitar

DAY 7

WEEK 1 TEST

Like I said, at the end of each week I'll be setting a few questions, just so you can check that the material you looked at over the course of the week is firmly entrenched. Here's the first.

1   What are the names of the guitar's open strings?

2   Which string is known as the 'bottom string'?

3   What is the left-hand thumb's main job?

4   Which part of the left-hand finger should be used to hold down the string?

5   What's another word for *plectrum*?

6   Which letter is used in a chord box to indicate an open string?

Acoustic Guitar

7 What does the word *arpeggio* mean?

8 If your chord changing is full of pauses, what can you do to correct this?

9 Where is the guitar's 'nut'?

10 What would the figure 'o' indicate on a line of tab?

WEEK 2

Welcome to Week 2. Hopefully everything is going well in the practice room and nothing is causing you undue distress. You may well be suffering a bit from sore fingers, but this can be considered par for the course, one aspect of the physical changes that guitar playing brings about, as predicted back in 'The Basics'. Rest assured that those fingertips will harden up after only a short while, and you won't feel a thing from then on!

Here are this week's objectives:

- To learn more about tuning;

- To wake up the left hand;

- To begin playing scales;

- To learn how to cross strings.

Acoustic Guitar

DAY 8: CHECK THAT TUNING

I said I was only going to nag you about tuning for a week, right? Well, today I'm not nagging, but I'm going to show you a method for checking how to check that the guitar is in tune with itself, while playing some more single notes.

QUOTE FOR THE DAY

Music is made up from harmony, melody and something extra to make it go...
– Frank Zappa

As you know by now, the task of tuning is one of the most important, especially in these early stages. Even though you've probably succumbed to my idea of an electronic tuner by now, it's still worth learning a method for checking the tuning of your guitar manually. You never know when you're going to need it, after all.

PRACTICAL EXERCISE

Basically, there are two types of tuning: making sure that your guitar is in tune with everyone else and making sure it's in tune with itself. This might sound a bit daft at first, but be patient. The guitar is a weird instrument, tuning-wise. When your learning becomes even more advanced, you'll discover that it's a physical impossibility for the guitar to be precisely in tune. (Several laws of physics actually make this so; it's not just something that's really tricky to pull off.) So, for now, just trust me that this method of checking what's known as *relative tuning* will pay off for you in the future. (Incidentally, I had a pupil once who thought that 'relative tuning' meant asking his uncle to tune his guitar for him. There's always one, eh?)

Acoustic Guitar

EXAMPLES

First of all, study the diagram below:

Track 9

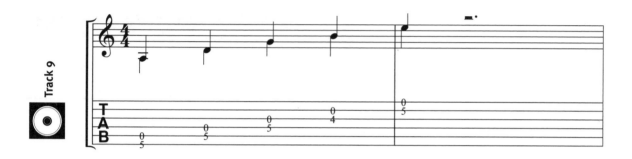

It's not really as complex as it looks, so don't panic. I'll talk you through it. First of all, I want you to make sure that your guitar is in tune. (It's far easier for you to see how this trick works when the guitar is already in tune. Trust me.) Now, play the note on the fifth fret, bass E string:

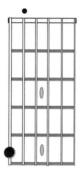

The note you're playing is an A, which is coincidentally the name of the open string next door (ie the A string). In actual fact, the two notes – the one you're playing and the open A string – should sound the same (now you see why it was vital that you tuned the guitar beforehand, right?). Play both of them together and listen hard: you should be able to hear that they're identical in pitch. If they aren't, check that you're reading the diagram correctly, and retune your guitar if necessary.

Now do the same for the A string. Play the note at the fifth fret and compare it to the open D string. Once again, both notes are Ds and should sound absolutely identical.

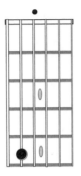

Now do the same for the D and G strings:

Now wait up, because things change a little for the G and B strings. Owing to the way the guitar is tuned, we find that the point at which the G and B strings agree in pitch is at the fourth fret, not the fifth, as shown here:

Acoustic Guitar

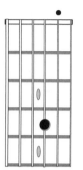

Play these two notes together – they should sound the same. Try to remember that it's these two strings that are the odd ones out (after all, there's a test at the end of the week, and this would be an obvious question for me to ask, wouldn't it?).

For the E and B strings, it's business as usual – back to the fifth fret for the *unison point*, which is just musicspeak for 'the point at which two or more notes are the same'.

Now repeat the whole exercise, one string at a time.

DAY 8 STUDY

Remember that each day's study period is effectively your workbench. I'm assuming that you haven't quite mastered last week's chords, so you should still go through them every day until you can literally play them with your eyes closed. Carry out the relative exercise every day, too – it's doing your music awareness (ie your ear training) an awful lot of good.

DAY 9: BRINGING THE LEFT-HAND FINGERS ONLINE

Today I'm going to let the rest of your left-hand fingers join in the fun and have a go at fretting some notes. This is going to be fairly hard going, depending on how useful your left hand is to you. If you're left-handed and have taken my advice to try to play the 'right-handed way' (as explained back in 'The Basics'), it's highly possible that you'll breeze through this week. If the most your left hand ever does is open the occasional door and change gear in your car, you could be in for a rough ride...

PRACTICAL EXERCISE

This lesson could take a lot of concentration, as it involves the start of a process that will begin to 'wake up' the muscles of the left-hand fingers and start training them up into the athletes they must become.

EXAMPLES

Take a look at the fretboard diagram below:

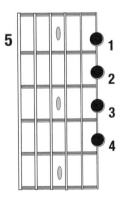

Here, all four of your left-hand fingers are lined up on a single string, holding it down together. This kind of thing might be something of a stretch for your left

hand, which is why I've written the exercise higher up the neck, where the frets are closer together.

Now take a very careful look at your left-hand thumb: it should be opposing the fingers and supporting them. Don't lay it down along the neck in either direction, as this will result in a loss of balance for the hand. Also, the fingers should be spread out, as shown in this photograph:

Left hand finger spread. This is the hand position that is the most practical for playing scales and melody parts, allowing one fret per finger

Note how the fingers lie close to the frets. This is because it's the fret that makes the note, and you need to position the fingers this close to make a good connection between the fret and the string, stopping it off. Don't pick any of the notes – in fact, give your right hand the day off; we'll concentrate on the left only today.

Now try to remove each of your left-hand fingers one at a time, like this:

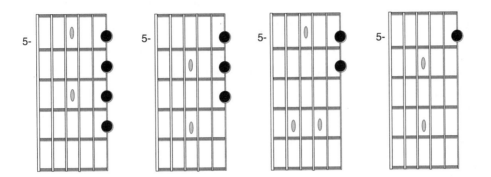

Leave the first finger in place and replace each of the fingers again, one by one.

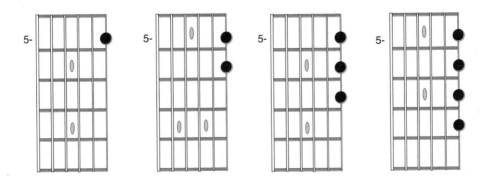

The chances are that chaos is going to reign here for a while and fingers are going to misbehave themselves to the extent that you're sure they're not actually connected to the mainframe. But be patient and remember that they have to learn to follow some pretty intricate instructions from here on – and it's only their second week at school!

Acoustic Guitar

How are last week's chords coming along? Hopefully, they're getting easier and more familiar with each passing day. The exercise we've been looking at today will help in that it will start to enliven those left-hand fingers even more. Meanwhile, carry out yesterday's little tuning exercise every day, too – you're creating some solid foundations here that we'll be building on in the weeks to come.

DAY 10: RIGHT- AND LEFT-HAND CO-ORDINATION

Today we're going to take a logical step forward from yesterday and play the notes in our left-hand line-up. This requires both left and right hands to work in perfect synchronisation, which in itself is not an easy trick to pull off. Just remember to take things slowly at this point in the course – and the best accompaniment for slow progress is patience!

PRACTICAL EXERCISE

It's probably better that you use a plectrum for today's exercise, as it's the best tool for getting a good, clear note on every occasion. If you're dead set against using one and have set your heart on being a pure fingerstylist, you can use your thumb. We'll be drilling the right-hand fingers into becoming a crack guitar-playing unit later on.

EXAMPLES

We'll look at today's exercise in tab, but just to save you turning the page unnecessarily, here's the fretboard diagram from yesterday, showing you where to place your left-hand fingers.

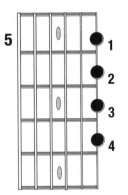

Now take a look at the tablature:

Acoustic Guitar

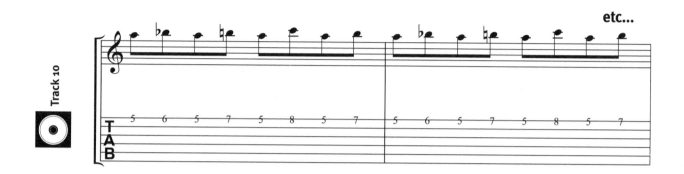

Track 10

You'll probably have gathered that it's a continuous exercise, despite the fact that I've written it out only twice, with a rather brave 'etc' at the end. I recommend that you aim to repeat this about ten times to begin with, stopping immediately if you find yourself getting cramp in your left hand. It's worth repeating that you're in the process of bringing muscles into play that have lain dormant all your life, and so you shouldn't be too surprised if they want to put up a bit of a fight in the meantime.

Now let's take a look at the right hand's role in all of this. After you're certain that you know exactly what the left hand is expected to do (this is why I introduced you to the role it plays here a day in advance), you should find that you can look away from the left hand and concentrate a little on the right.

Play each of the notes with a downstroke of the pick (or thumb) one at a time, *dead slow*. I want you to play this no faster than one note per second (if you've got a clock around the house that ticks fairly loudly, this will give you an accurate idea of what I mean – one note per tick is your absolute speed limit), even if you think you're capable of it. The example on the CD should give you an idea of what the exercise should sound like.

DAY 10 STUDY

While you're working through this exercise, stop occasionally and ask yourself these questions:

- Where's my left-hand thumb? Is it in the middle of the guitar neck, supporting the fingers correctly?

- Is there any unwanted tension in my left arm?

- Am I tensing my left shoulder unnecessarily?

- Is my right arm tense or relaxed?

- Does each note sound as clear as the last, or should I be looking for gremlins?

If you find that any of the notes you're producing are muted or buzzy, remember to check that the fingers are making a perfect 'lock' with the string and fretboard and that the finger concerned is at the back of the fret, effecting a good contact. Meanwhile, keep cracking on with those chords from last week – you'll be expanding your chordal repertoire next week!

Acoustic Guitar

DAY 11: THEME AND VARIATION

In order that the left-hand fingers really start to hear their wake up call, it's necessary to keep throwing new things at them. I don't expect yesterday's exercise to sound perfect quite yet – that's what the practice workbench is for – but in the meantime we're going to throw a variation at those left-hand fingers, just to make sure they're concentrating. As for the right hand, you'll be glad to know that everything is going to stay the same for today, so you have another day's grace for getting your plucking or picking action honed to perfection – or thereabouts.

PRACTICAL EXERCISE

Basically, what we're going to do today is alter the order in which the left-hand fingers play the notes from yesterday's exercise. But before we do so, a few words about anatomy...

I've already forewarned you that your body is going to have to adapt to the physical demands that guitar playing places upon it, and one of the first examples of this concerns the independence of your fingers. When the hand was originally blueprinted, it was thought that it would be used for pretty ordinary stuff: holding tools, picking fruit and the general day-to-day stuff of basic existence. Since then, of course, we've had to adapt to things like holding pencils, opening those annoying milk cartons you buy in supermarkets and other evolutionary necessities along the way. Guitar playing was never part of The Grand Design for the human race, and so we can expect to come across a few glitches along the way where expectations exceed the original design initiative.

Try this experiment: lay your left hand flat on a table or desk and try to raise each of your fingers individually. First, raise the index finger, leaving the others flat on the table. Not too hard, eh? Now try the second finger – bit tricky? What about

the third? My bet is that when you tried to raise it, leaving the others flat on the deck, you either couldn't or the little finger wanted to lift, too.

This is not your fault, or your hand's; it's anatomy, and we can't do a thing but train the disobedient digits concerned to do what we want. This is why you might find these initial forays into left-hand independence difficult at first – it's something that the hand has to learn, and the only control you have over the situation is to be a patiently persistent teacher and literally let nature take its course. It's not something that you'll never be able to do, if you'll forgive the double negative...

EXAMPLES

Enough said about anatomy. On to the examples themselves.

Track 11

Here's the first variation on the four-finger exercise we looked at yesterday. Nothing's changed except the order in which you play the notes; your hand position remains the same, and the right-hand picking regime is identical. Your only task is to get those fingers on your left hand to obey the orders spouting from your brain!

Acoustic Guitar

Two variations? Afraid so. Seriously, one isn't enough; you need to alter the order of the fingers at least a couple of times for the full benefit of this lesson to take hold.

You don't need me to tell you that this is a bit of a monster, and you certainly won't be able to tame it in a single day, but by keeping it in your practice routine you'll be doing some valuable work that will set the hand up ready for the next level.

DAY 11 STUDY

By now, you've got quite a few things to fix on the practice workbench – all those chords from last week and all the melody exercises from this week – but don't labour too long and hard; a little practice on a daily basis is the best thing at this stage. Your worst enemies at this point are boredom, frustration and fatigue, and so little and often is the way to go.

DAY 12: CROSSING STRINGS

Today we'll be taking a look at the next major task in melody playing: changing strings. Until now, you've been playing melody lines on single strings, which is obviously not the way things are done out there in the real world. You've got six strings, so let's use them!

PRACTICAL EXERCISE

For this exercise, we're going to compromise a little in that I want you to move down the neck to the lower frets. However, because the frets are wider apart down here – which will impose more of a demand on your fingers – we're going to play only five notes. Deal?

EXAMPLES

If you're looking for some kind of benchmark, today is the first time you'll play some melody notes that actually have some musical meaning. Exercises are renowned for sounding ugly and non-melodic, but this one sounds a lot better. Of course, you don't get anything for nothing in this world, so you're going to have to work a bit first.

Repeat...

Acoustic Guitar

Look at the exercise on the previous page. It's down on the fourth and fifth strings, covering a span of four frets, from the second to the fifth. The fretboard diagram below shows the notes you'll be covering:

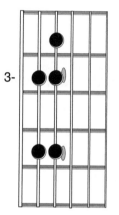

The main factor of awkwardness here is that your hand is going to feel a bit stretched because you're reaching further over the fretboard than before. So far, we've really covered only the first three strings, and you'll probably be surprised by how different the neck 'feels' just by stretching the hand over a little bit more. It's worth making this particular journey now, though, because the sooner you have the entire width of the guitar fretboard available to you, the better.

Chances are you're going to get into another 'rubberneck' situation with this exercise, because not only do your fretting fingers have to negotiate a string change but your picking hand does too, so for a while there's going to be a bit of looking from one to the other and back to the book as you carry out the basic navigation for this particular exercise. Take your time – it's a lesson best learnt slowly – and don't allow yourself to become frustrated if the basic synchronisation between left and right hands isn't there from the outset. It will soon come. (Incidentally, you've just played the beginning of your first musical scale – C major, to be precise.)

DAY 12 STUDY

Today's study is in the form of a brain teaser designed to test your sense of co-ordination on the fretboard. If you look at the scale fragment we've been studying, you'll notice that it goes from the third fret on the A string to the fifth fret on the D. Look at the fretboard diagram and compare the overview it presents with what's actually happening. Try to put the exercise together from the fretboard diagram alone, covering up the tablature if necessary. Turn the whole thing into a game and see if you can put things back together from just the diagram.

When you've got it, play the whole thing backwards. Start at the last note on the diagram (ie fret 5, D string) and play down to the first.

Acoustic Guitar

DAY 13: SCALING THE HEIGHTS

We might as well round off Week 2's lessons with something really significant, so let's play a whole scale.

If you've ever played any other musical instrument, you'll probably remember that many of the early days are spent practising scales. You might also remember how boring that is, too. But when you consider that scales are a bit like learning the musical alphabet, it kind of puts things into perspective. I know they can be a chore – and I'm going to try to keep them to a minimum in this book – but they're also necessary, and they are absolutely the best vehicle to train those flailing digits of yours into the SWAT team they need to become.

PRACTICAL EXERCISE

The good news is that your left-hand little finger gets the day off today! If there is any bad news, then I suppose it would be that there's an awful lot more string crossing to be done in this exercise.

EXAMPLES

There are also going to be some open strings included in the tablature. (Remember that these are marked with an 'o' on the tab.) So let's get down to business.

Track 13

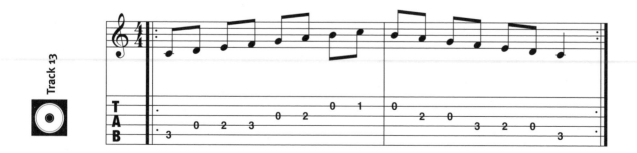

Don't worry, it's not half as bewildering as it looks. The most important thing here is the discipline involving the left-hand fingers. Obviously, when we play melody on the guitar, we want to do so in the most economical and practical way. If fingering is allowed to become random, it can be completely chaotic on the fingerboard, so we need some kind of system. Here, the fingering isn't hard to remember, because you'll be using this basic plan:

Third-fret notes = third finger
Second-fret notes = second finger
First-fret notes = first finger

Hopefully, you'll agree that this is quite a logical and easy pattern to commit to memory. You'll probably find that it also helps a great deal if you say the fingering out loud; for some reason, this means you end up absorbing it a lot quicker.

Start off with your third finger on the third fret of the fifth string and then pluck the open fourth string. Don't take your hand away from the neck just because there are no left-hand fingers involved; leave it in position so that it's ready to play the next note immediately. Economy of movement is, as I've said, an important discipline.

For this exercise, you're playing the scale of C major in both directions, and it's important, for the general musicality of the proceedings, for all the notes involved to be evenly spaced. Play the exercise through slowly, aiming for a kind of basic 'beat', even if it's really, dead slow. If you learn to practise things evenly at this stage, you'll be able to speed them up later on. If the basic clockwork is solid, you're really on the right track.

DAY 13 STUDY

We'll round off this week's lessons with another little challenge. Over the last couple of days, you've played two different versions of the same thing: the C major scale. Yesterday's version was a fragment and at a different place on the

Acoustic Guitar

fretboard, and today's was the whole scale, up and down. What I want you to do now is compare the two and see if they share any characteristics. The fingering is different, but perhaps they sound very similar?

Incidentally, if you're into trivia and want something musically knowledgeable to drop into a conversation sometime, the word *scale* comes from the Latin word *scalae*, meaning 'ladder'. It's not a bad way to think about them, either; if you consider that scales are musical ladders that are used in the construction of melodies, then you're definitely thinking along the right lines!

Acoustic Guitar

DAY 14

WEEK 2 TEST

Here's another teaser to tax your brain. All the answers are in the previous week's lessons, so if you're not sure about anything, jolly well go back and check!

1 What are the two basic types of tuning?

2 What's the note found at the fifth fret, bass E string, called?

3 What's the note found at the fifth fret, A string, called?

4 Which pair of strings defeats the 'fifth-fret tuning' strategy?

5 Why is it best to put your left-hand finger as close as possible to a fret when sounding a string?

6 What's the value of doing left-hand exercises further up the neck, away from the nut?

Acoustic Guitar

7 If a note sounds unclear or fuzzy, what's your prime suspect?

8 What's anatomy's role in left-hand development?

9 What's the name of the scale fragment you learned this week?

10 What does the word *scale* actually mean?

WEEK 3

Welcome to Week 3. This week, we're going to expand your knowledge of chords a little and make fuller use of the fretboard whilst doing so.

Your objectives for this week are:

- To learn how to use six string chords;

- To make chord changes more efficient;

- To learn how to arpeggiate chords;

- To start using a plectrum.

Acoustic Guitar

DAY 15: GROWN-UP CHORDS

So far, the chords I've shown you cover only the first three strings, which is all fine and dandy, but wouldn't they sound a lot fuller if we employed the fourth, fifth and sixth strings, too? Of course they would, so let's give it a go.

PRACTICAL EXERCISE

As you learned last week, using more of the fretboard carries with it a few physical challenges for the left hand. (How's it holding up, incidentally? If you've got peeling skin on your fingertips and the occasional ache in the muscle between left-hand forefinger and thumb, things are progressing nicely!) This week, we'll look at a series of much fuller-sounding chords that use more of the left-hand fingers. Fear not, though, I'll try to do things in the proper order so that the demands placed on your left hand are pretty gradual.

EXAMPLES

The first of these new chords is called *E minor*, and it uses two left-hand fingers...and all six strings!

Track 14

92

You'll probably agree that everything sounds a little more rock 'n' roll now that we're using some bass strings, but how are the notes you're holding down doing? It could just be that four out of the six are sounding fine, but the two being held by your left-hand fingers are a little muted. In order to check whether or not this is so, try this test: hold down the chord as shown in the previous diagram and sound each string one at a time, starting with the bass E string. When you arrive at the fifth and fourth strings, double-check to make sure that both fingers are seated right and aren't obviously 'overhanging' onto neighbouring strings, then play them. If they still sound muted, unclear or just plain strange, take a deep breath and work through the following checklist...

1 Is your thumb in the right position

2 Are your fingers connecting with the strings by their tips?

3 Is your left arm as relaxed as possible, without the elbow sticking up in the air?

...and try again. Honestly, if you get this kind of thing sorted out now, your fingers will learn their job that much quicker and more efficiently. Believe it or not, fingers have a kind of 'touch memory' that helps them remember what works and what doesn't, and you'll soon pick it up with a little bit of patience.

DAY 15 STUDY

This week is going to be all about chords, but don't let those scale exercises slip! You've got a week to get them out on the workbench and really give them a good old workout while you're busy learning chords. So, seeing as this week we're standing still, as far as melody is concerned, take advantage of the chance to polish your melody exercises to a shine.

Acoustic Guitar

DAY 16: TWO-FINGER BALLET CLASS

I'm aware that yesterday might have posed a new set of challenges, in that it takes a while for the practice of playing chords that require multiple fingers to feel and sound natural. The trouble is, everything will feel strange to you during these early days, and it's difficult to know if things are going as well as perhaps they might. Keep comparing what you're playing with the examples on the CD, and only move forward on any of the exercises once you're absolutely sure that things are really up and running.

Yesterday you made a start on your new chord collection, and we're going to be building on it over the next few days. It's a fact that a guitarist spends most of his or her time playing chords, so this is all very important stuff.

It's not uncommon at this point for someone to ask the question 'Well, how many chords are there?' The answer is 'Lots!', but the good news is that you don't need to know all of them, by any means. You can actually get by quite well knowing comparatively few chords, in much the same way that you can hold a perfectly fine conversation without needing all the words in a dictionary.

Over the next few days we're going to tackle the job of learning chords in the most logical fashion, introducing two-, then three- and finally four-finger chords so that the hands and ears have the optimum chance to learn this new information at a sensible rate.

EXAMPLES

I'm going to introduce you to three more chords today. Don't worry if you think we're moving too fast; just remember that everything you're learning here should be allotted time on the practice workbench. Spend enough time with it there and

it will soon filter down to your memory and you'll be performing these chords
with ease.

Track 15

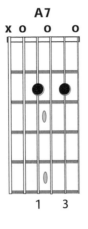

Here's the first new chord. It's called A7 and, once again, uses only two fingers –
although now we're bringing left-hand finger number 3 into play. Of course, you
could play the chord using fingers 1 and 2 – there aren't really any hard-and-fast
rules about this, just recommendations and suggestions. I suggest, for instance,
that you try it with fingers 1 and 3, if only because it's a good idea to introduce a
new finger into the equation at this time. Also...

- Remember to apply the 'one string at a time' rule and run down the checklist if
  anything sounds muted or blurry.

- Make sure that you observe the little 'x' over the sixth string, which means
  that only five strings are needed in this particular chord.

Acoustic Guitar

Our second chord is called E7 and once again employs left-hand fingers 1 and 3. This time, you've got all six strings to play, but watch out for string number 4 – the D string – because its position between the two strings that your fingers are on make it a prime candidate for being muted. If this is the case, reposition your fingers until everything is ringing loud and clear. Don't proceed until it is!

The final new chord of today is known as A minor seventh – a bit of a mouthful, and quite often abbreviated to Amin7 when it's written down. You'll notice straight away, I expect, that it's the same general shape as E7 but located on a different pair of strings. The same rules apply here as before: check each string

independently and make sure everything is ringing as it should, performing a little finger ballet if something sounds amiss.

DAY 16 STUDY

Remember the chord exercise we had back in the early days? Well, we're going to put another one together here. (I expect you were getting bored with the other one, in any case.) As before, I've written it out in the form of a chord chart for you to follow – and, despite the fact that I've written it out only once, I would advise you to play it through at least five to ten times per day, just to make sure it really has the chance to bed in.

| Emin / / / | E7 / / / | Amin7 / / / | A7 / / / ||

As far as chord exercises go, this one doesn't sound too bad. Just in case you feel inspired to write a song using it, and it becomes a Number One single, don't forget where you saw it first…

Track 15

Acoustic Guitar

DAY 17: CHANGE PARTNERS!

The chances are that yesterday's chord exercise was a little frustrating, in that it takes time to change over from one chord to the next, so if the result sounded hesitant and jerky, don't worry – it will take time to smooth out the changes. You'll soon be moving from one to the next with the sure-footed agility of a mountain goat, fear not.

PRACTICAL EXERCISE

As far as chord changes go, here are a few guidelines that might just help you to streamline what you've been doing so far. The most important of these is to understand exactly where a chord change takes place. Now, you might be thinking that the answer here is an obvious one, in that chord changes take place on the fretboard, right? Wrong. A successful chord change actually takes place in mid-air.

EXAMPLES

Let's take a close look at what happens when we change between two of the chords in our repertoire. I nominate Emin to Amin7:

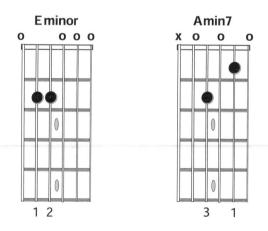

Here are the chord boxes once again, just to refresh your memory and save those time-wasting page turns. And here's the job in hand:

| Em / / / | Amin7 / / / ||

The task begins with E minor, using left-hand fingers 1 and 2. After strumming it four times, we move to a different pair of strings, lose the second left-hand finger and deploy the third instead – and it's all got to happen here:

*
| Em / / / | Amin7 / / / ||

If it doesn't, the flow is lost and we introduce a bump into an otherwise smooth rhythmic surface.

When you think about it, quite a lot has to happen at this vital point. I'm monumentally hopeless at maths, but it's not beyond even me to work out that if the tempo of the song you're playing (I know it's not a song, it's an exercise, but humour me just this once, OK?) was 60 beats per minute – slow by musical standards – then you'd have to carry out this finger manoeuvre in the space of one second. As I said, 60 beats per minute is slow, and so the time is only going to get shorter – at 120 beats per minute (which is considered a moderate tempo in music circles) you'd have only half a second, so you can see how important it is to get this basic feat sorted out here and now.

So what exactly did I mean when I said that an efficient chord change actually takes place in mid-air? What I'm saying is that the one place that all the necessary finger choreography involved in changing chords *shouldn't* take place is on the fingerboard, because it's already too late to meddle around once the fingers have landed. You want them to land together, already in position and on the beat, and so the shape-swap has to happen in mid-air between the chords. See what I mean? The fingers leave the E minor chord, and before they're replaced on the fingerboard they've already assumed the shape of the Amin7 chord, ready for a perfect landing.

Acoustic Guitar

Obviously, this isn't a skill that happens suddenly; it's something that needs to be worked on slowly and methodically, so today's study requires you to take the chord exercise from yesterday (the one your first hit single is going to be based upon) and work out how these mid-air changes happen. Here it is once again, so you don't have to turn pages:

| Eminor / / / | E7 / / / | Amin7 / / / | A7 / / / ||

Study exactly what has to happen with your left hand when you move between each of the chords. Try to visualise the shape of the new chord and 'morph' the fingers into the new shape mid-change.

DAY 18: SOME THREE-FINGER CHORDS

! I know that what we've looked at so far is building up into a pretty intensive practice schedule, and it's possible that you're wondering how you're going to fit it all in. I've believed for a long time that a great deal can be achieved in a surprisingly short space of time, and that sometimes putting a time limit on an exercise actually encourages people to play it better! So don't spend too long on any one exercise when you sit down to practise; try to spread things out as evenly as possible. The material that you're sure of can be safely placed on the practice back-burner for a while as you deal with the newer and more unfamiliar tasks in hand. Divide things up successfully in this way and you're guaranteed to make progress.

PRACTICAL EXERCISE

Unsurprisingly, today I'm going to introduce you to some three-finger chords. Your first is a familiar one, an enlarged version of C major:

Now, I know that all we're doing here is introducing another finger into the equation, but I'd better warn you about something else that's happening, too. We've already seen how the hands have to adapt to the demands of the guitar,

Acoustic Guitar

and what you'll very probably experience with the C major chord is that the span of your left hand isn't quite full enough to accommodate it the first time. In other words, it feels like your third finger really has to stretch to make it to the third fret, fifth string. What's more, you've still got to make sure that fingers 1 and 2 are holding up their part of the bargain, too.

Now, you know I'm going to tell you that this is just another bridge to cross and that patience will conquer all, don't you? Well, it's absolutely true, and, what's more, the hand has to stretch this distance only a few times before the whole fretboard is at your command. So take things slowly, try to understand that your body has to undergo another morphic feat, and be patient while it happens!

EXAMPLES

While we're here, I'm going to give you another couple of chords that call for the left hand to spend time on the rack:

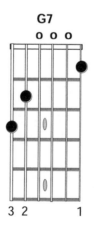

Firstly, here's G7 – and no, you're not hallucinating, it really does call for the second finger to hold down the fifth string.

To make things easier, I'll say that the job for today is merely to navigate your way through these new three-finger chords and not necessarily to play them in

any context quite yet. Remember to apply the same basic checklist as before –
the chances are that the third finger will want to lean on string 5 and mute it, but
you must try very hard to see to it that this doesn't happen.

This is the cruellest of all today's chords, calling for you to stretch your second
finger over to string 6 while fingers 1 and 3 hold down strings 5 and 1
respectively. The problem is usually the third finger; despite the fact that it
doesn't have to stretch like fingers 1 and 2, it's still in one heck of an awkward
position, tucked away almost into the palm. If it refuses point-blank to follow
orders, there's no harm in using your right hand to pull it gently into position –
and I mean, of course, gently. When your hand 'feels' what needs to be done, it
will learn the necessary basic movements far more quickly.

DAY 18 STUDY

Today's little workout has more to do with calisthenics than with actual music.
It's giving you a chance to explore slowly and methodically some of the extreme
movements your left-hand fingers have to perform, in advance of the time when
you're actually going to need to put these particular chords into context. It would
actually help you to understand what I mean if you think of it in terms of yoga!

Acoustic Guitar

Track 16

| Gmaj / / / | G7 / / / | Cmaj / / / | Cmaj / / / ||

The exercise above contains the same chords, but this is the order in which I want you to perform them. It means even more of an aerial ballet than before – look at the movement necessary between the G major and G7 chords, for instance, and choreograph your fingers to make that change happen in mid-air – but be sure to take things dead slow. Imagine that you're involved in a slow-motion sequence in a movie and you'll have an appropriate frame of reference.

DAY 19: ARPEGGIATING THOSE NEW SHAPES

You've really got your hands full at the moment, dealing with yesterday's stretchy chord shapes. Well, when I say 'hands full', I guess it's only really the left hand that's preoccupied, going through another metamorphosis, while the right hand is really just strumming along as usual. Until now, that is...

In order that you have more time for the left hand to get its fingers behaving themselves, now's a good time to introduce some right-hand tasks. For these, you'll be using either a plectrum or your thumb (although a plectrum is better) to arpeggiate some of the chords you've been wrestling with.

PRACTICAL EXERCISE

Today's examples give you the opportunity to see some of the ways we can use chords to make things sound more interesting. After all, a strummed chord is a strummed chord – that's where it stops, and it's not necessarily the most interesting thing you can do in a song or instrumental passage. Returning to the idea of arpeggiating chords, you'll find that we can make things sound way more interesting without an awful lot more effort.

EXAMPLES

Until now, our attempts at arpeggiating have been all well and good, but they haven't been particularly organised. When we strum chords, we do so in such a way that they're played the same number of times (ie there are the same number of *beats*) in each bar:

|| Cmaj / / / | G7 / / / ||

The above example requires you to play each of the chords four times, which means that the rhythm of whatever it is you're playing remains constant. If you

Acoustic Guitar

played five strums per bar here and four there, things would sound very directionless and muddled, and so the aim is to try to make sure that everything is even and in order.

If you were to pull the same sort of rhythmic etiquette off with arpeggiated patterns, you'd have to make sure that everything was balanced there, too. So let's take the C major chord and give it some kind of rhythmic arpeggio:

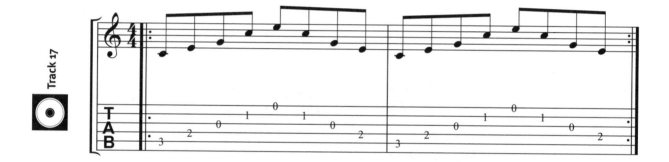

Track 17

Take a look at the example above. The tab is telling you to play the C chord as individual notes with the right hand. This still means that you lay all the left hand fingers down on the neck simultaneously, just as you would if you were strumming. (Don't be tempted to try to lay them down one at a time, even though that's what the tab appears to be asking you to do.) You'll see that you're playing the fifth string, followed by the fourth, third, second and first and back again, and when you do so, things take on a certain rhythmic continuity. If I wrote down what's going on from a music point of view, we'd come up with this:

| 1 & 2 & 3 & 4 & | 1 & 2 & 3 & 4 & ||

You appear to be playing eight beats to the bar, but in fact you're not; you're playing four beats to the bar, but each of them has been sliced in two. And so, instead of counting our way through things by saying aloud, 'One, two, three,

Acoustic Guitar

four', as we have been when we've been strumming our way through the previous chord exercises, this time you're saying, '*One* and *two* and *three* and *four* and'. This keeps everything metrically neat and tidy and in perfect rhythm – exactly what's needed for accompanying a song or melody. Don't concern yourself too much at this point with why this happens to be so; just put it down to the fact that music insists upon things being symmetrically valid like this and, for now, take things at face value.

If you're using a plectrum to play this exercise, try to use downstrokes all the way across and back. I'll introduce you to another way of doing things tomorrow.

DAY 19 STUDY

The only thing you have to add to your practice routine today is this idea for playing the C chord as an arpeggio, as opposed to a single strum. Holding down a single chord while the right hand comes to terms with picking each individual string gives you the opportunity to focus more fully on processing the new information. Let the left hand have an easy time of it for a change as the right hand gets a grip on some new technique. Play it through like this...

...and spend at least a couple of minutes on it, making sure that the right hand is doing exactly what's expected of it.

Acoustic Guitar

DAY 20: PLECTRUM ATHLETICS!

Hopefully, you were able to synchronise things yesterday so that you ended up with a good, evenly spaced arpeggio like the one on the accompanying CD. Today, we're going to fine-tune your right-hand technique for playing arpeggios a little bit, so that the job becomes more logical.

You really will be better off using a plectrum for today's exercise, as playing it with your thumb won't really work. This is because we're going to discover how to go about playing an upstroke with the pick – and that's not an easy trick to perform using your thumb.

PRACTICAL EXERCISE

Until now, your plectrum strokes have all been going one way – that is, they've essentially been starting above a string, plucking it and following through in a downwards motion, towards the floor. This kind of plectrum action is universally known as *playing downstrokes* with the pick, and it's really only half the story as far as proper picking is concerned. It won't come as too much of a surprise to hear that the other type of pick stroke is the exact reverse and is known as an *upstroke*.

If you think about it, it's entirely logical that you should make full use of the natural up-and-down movement of the plectrum. After all, when you strum a chord, the pick has to travel upwards before you can perform your next downstroke, so why waste this action? Let's make every move of the hand count, if we can.

EXAMPLES

In order to start you off on the road to up-and-down strumming, it's probably best that you try things out on open strings first so that you can pay 100% attention to what your right hand is doing without having to worry about what the left hand is getting up to.

Acoustic Guitar

First of all, imagine you're going to use up- and downstrokes on a chord. Yesterday we came across a way of playing eight strokes to the bar instead of four by counting 'one and two and three and four and', so let's see how this translates into a picking regime. Try a basic strum using an upstroke, to begin with – you might be able to tell that it doesn't sound the same as it would with a downstroke. There are a couple of reasons for this, not least of which is the fact that you're playing the notes of the chord in a different order! The other reason is slightly more subtle, but important all the same. It's really all to do with gravity…

When you play a downstroke, you've got the whole weight of your hand behind the stroke, which has the effect of making it sound quite dynamic. However, when you try an upstroke, you're fighting against the weight of the hand, making it sound slightly weaker. Add to this the fact that any chord heard 'upside-down' – ie with the high notes on top played first and the bass following on behind – sounds typically weaker, too, and you've instantly got two different chordal textures under your hand.

So, if we play our way through a bar of music like this…

```
| 1     &    2     &    3     &    4     & |
| down  up   down  up   down  up   down  up |
```

…we've got the stronger sound of the chord in the right place: on the main beats, as opposed to the 'and's. As I've said, I don't want you to worry about why this should be so; it's just one of music's little quirks that you'll find out all about later on. For now, just experiment with the ups and downs of picking life and leave it at that.

Acoustic Guitar

Now let's apply this kind of up-and-down thinking to picking yesterday's arpeggio. This is an awkward thing to perform accurately, but it's good to pull it out onto the practice workbench at this stage in order to make sure it has the optimum chance to work its way into your playing over time.

It's important that you play through this exercise using strict alternate picking, playing the first note as a downstroke. It will probably help if you say out loud to yourself, 'Down, up, down, up,' etc, because it will help you to keep the exercise in focus.

This is another exercise that will have to be played dead slow to begin with – and promise me that you won't even attempt to speed it up until you're absolutely sure that the basic mechanics are all in place. If you try to speed something up that still has a few bugs left in it, you'll have less chance of ever achieving the type of accuracy you need. It's at least twice as hard to go back and put something right later on as it is to get it right in the first place!

Acoustic Guitar

DAY 21

WEEK 3 TEST

Time for another test, I think. Work your way through carefully, and be sure not to move on until you can answer all of the questions listed below.

---

1   Is A7 a five- or six-string chord?

2   What is the accepted abbreviation for an A minor seventh chord?

3   Where does an efficient chord change actually take place?

4   What might be the initial problem with the full C major chord?

5   Which left-hand finger might put up the most resistance to the G major chord?

6   What are the two types of plectrum stroke known as?

Acoustic Guitar

7   What's the minimum gauge of plectrum you should consider for playing
    individual notes? (You'll need to look this up back in 'The Basics' if you
    haven't already read it.)

8   Why is there a difference in sound between upstrokes and downstrokes when
    playing a chord?

9   What happens to the beat when eight notes are played per bar?

10 Which string does the C major arpeggio start with?

WEEK 4

Welcome to Week 4. You're nearly halfway through your crash course in acoustic-guitar playing, and the foundations we've been digging together should now mean that your skills are developing nicely. You've got the basic idea about playing chords, playing melody notes, using alternate picking with a plectrum and much more besides. This week, we'll be adding to those skills by taking a look at basic fingerpicking, including:

- Digging deep foundations for fingerstyle playing;

- Learning fingerpicked arpeggios.

Acoustic Guitar

DAY 22: OPEN-STRING FANDANGO

As I've said, your choice of how to sound the strings is basically restricted to two options: with a plectrum or by fingerpicking. In the end, you'll probably find that one or the other suits you better and decide to specialise accordingly, but for now it's a good idea to familiarise yourself with the basics of both so that you have the broadest possible foundations to build on whichever style of playing you choose.

" QUOTE FOR THE DAY

A piece of music could come from two chords that sound good together. Then it's up to you to unravel the rest.

– Dominic Miller

EXAMPLES

First of all, let's examine the fundamentals of fingerpicking. Traditionally, your right-hand fingers are assigned letters, like this:

p = thumb
i = index
m = middle
a = ring

You don't use your right-hand little finger (although in some extreme circles of classical playing this is becoming more and more common) because it's not particularly strong and way too short.

As to which fingers look after which strings, it's not really set in stone, but in general it tends to be the case that the thumb looks after the bass strings – that's the E, A and D strings – and the index, middle and ring fingers look after the top three treble strings.

So let's get down to business. Try this basic orienteering exercise: place your thumb on the fifth string, index finger on the G, middle finger on the B and ring finger on the top E:

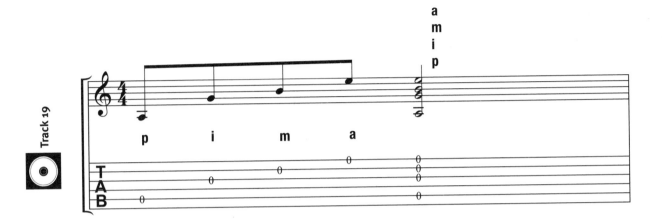

Track 19

Now, follow the tab and play through this:

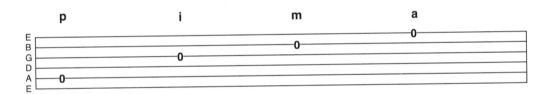

You're playing only open strings, so there's nothing for the left hand to do as yet. Once again, it's important to do things this way around so that your focus is 100% on the hand learning the new technique. Listen to the CD as a reference for what the exercise should sound like.

DAY 22 STUDY

There should be quite a lot on your practice workbench as we sail into Week 4 of this course. You should be constantly reviewing everything we've done so far because it will all help to develop the technique necessary to take you forward into the forthcoming lessons. For today, though, it's time to get those right-hand fingers working on the strings, and so I'll add one variation to the exercise we've looked at already. Here are both together:

CRASH COURSE

Acoustic Guitar

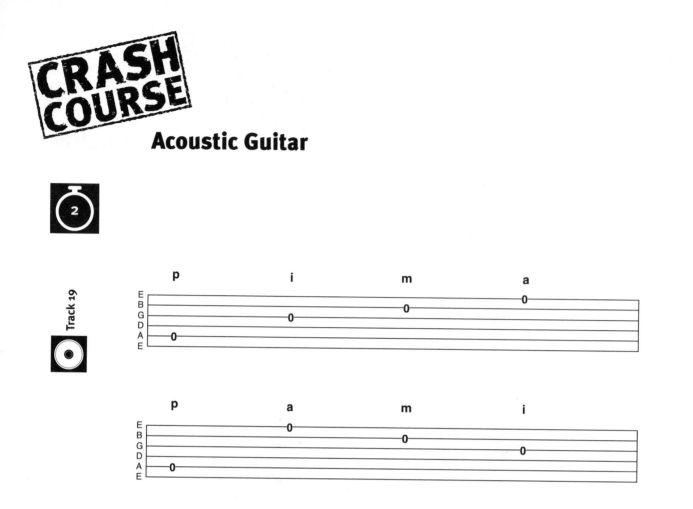

In the first exercise, you're playing from the bass strings over to the top, but in the second you're playing the strings top to bottom. Play both exercises for a minute each and then move on to the rest of your practice routine.

DAY 23: MAKING IT MUSICAL

Today we'll take a closer look at what we started yesterday and examine the technique necessary to develop a good, solid fingerstyle technique.

Let's re-examine what's going on with your right hand fingers. First of all, it's going to be necessary to talk a little about an age-old debate that's been smouldering in the shadows of fingerstyle guitar for many years: flesh or nail? Now, this is a question that's more relevant to classical-guitar technique, but I feel I must make you aware of it, as it will broaden your horizons a little more and present you with a couple of alternatives to consider.

With nylon-string guitar, these days it's pretty commonplace for a guitarist to use his or her fingernail to sound the string, but at one time there was a question as to whether fingernail or fingertip flesh gave the better sound. Both are possible while each presents a slightly different tone, and, as I say, for some time a furious debate raged in the normally quiet circles of classical guitar regarding this question. As far as we metal-string players are concerned, we have the same choice but one more thing to take into consideration: steel strings can tear the average fingernail to pieces in a very short while.

Fingernail strength differs from person to person. I've known people whose fingernails actually flake away at the mere introduction of a guitar string, while others have veritable talons at the ends of their fingers. I'm lucky because I fall into this second category, so I can play with my fingernails without taking on too much damage. I actually use my thumbnail to open those cellophane wrappers record companies insist on putting around CD cases. Grrrr...

Just to prove to you how important the issue fingernails can be amongst professional guitarists, I know of two top players who employ the strengthening power of nail varnish and other proprietary applications just to ensure that their nails remain up to the task while on tour.

Acoustic Guitar

So what does all this mean to you? Do you need to grow some claws to make your guitar growl? Well, no, not really. Even if you do end up deciding to play fingerstyle exclusively, you might only need to grow your right-hand fingernails so that there's just a little bit of white showing right at the end. You certainly won't need to end up looking like Freddy Krueger, don't worry. Whatever happens, you'll need to make sure that the string travels across the tip of your finger, which means that you'll have to employ a hand position very like the one shown in this picture:

Right-hand fingerstyle. In essence, the thumb looks after the bass strings and the fingers look after the top three strings, as shown here

You can see that here the fingers are curled over the strings, ready to play with the tips, whether there's a nail there or not. It might feel a little strange at first, but make sure that your hand isn't cramped up or clawed because that's an invitation to our old enemy, tension, which will slow all your fingerstyle efforts to an absolute crawl.

EXAMPLES

Right, so we've discussed fingernails and right-hand position. Now here's something to play. First of all, let's put yesterday's exercise to a more musical use by introducing a chord in the right hand:

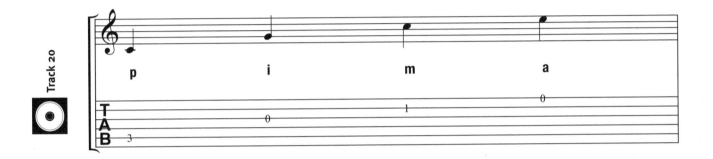

It's the C major chord that we've been seeing quite a lot of lately, and so this shouldn't introduce too dangerous a learning curve to the exercise as your left hand should now know the chord position well. Once again, we'll play it both up and down, but this time I'll turn the whole return journey into a single exercise:

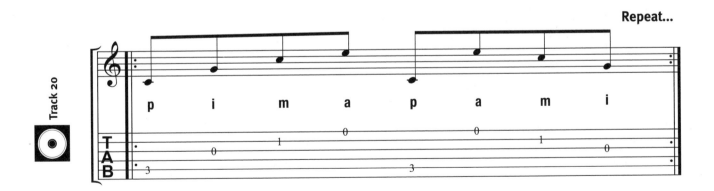

Remember to take it slowly. Yes, I know I keep reminding you, but you'd probably be surprised how many times I have to keep telling the people I teach to keep within their individual speed limits in order to prevent things from falling to pieces, which happens rather quickly if they don't.

Acoustic Guitar

DAY 23 STUDY

For today's study, I'm going to ask you to adopt the fingerstyle method while playing a couple of the other chords we've looked at in the past. All I want you to do is apply the same set of rules as before: keep it slow and make it as clean as possible.

Track 20

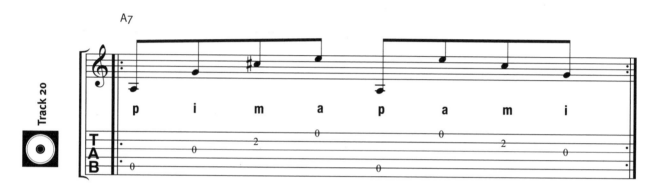

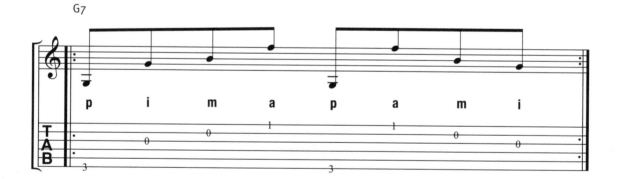

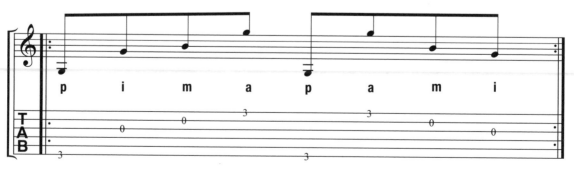

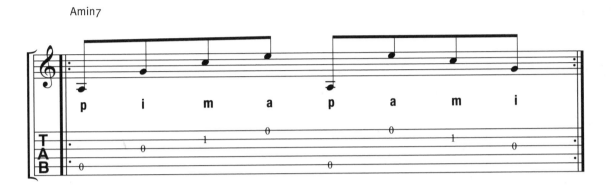

Just play through each example a few times. We're really just introducing the right-hand fingers to this type of playing, and they've already got quite a lot to absorb, so we'll go easy on them. There's time to work that body later on!

Acoustic Guitar

DAY 24: FINGERSTYLE VARIATIONS

You probably saw this one coming. Until now, you've been playing chords across from the bass to treble strings and back again, but of course this is only one way of doing things. There are plenty of variations available to us, so let's look at a couple of them.

PRACTICAL EXERCISE

I like to think of this sort of thing as being the equivalent of tongue twisters for the fingers. By introducing a different order to the playing of the strings, we are increasing our digits' aptitude and usefulness. There's a book by Mauro Giuliani that's popular in classical guitar circles because it's full of variations for the right-hand fingers, just to ensure that they can cope with anything they're called upon to do. Of course, we're not going to go that far; we're digging foundations here, and that kind of refinement is a course you're welcome to take later on if you wish. For now, we'll look at just a few different picking patterns as a drill for the fingers. The idea here is that they should be able to adapt themselves much easier to just about any variation after doing a bit of work now.

EXAMPLES

First of all, let's look once again at our C major chord. Remember that keeping the left hand on solid ground like this makes it easier to focus on the shock of the new stuff that's going on with your right. Take a look at the following exercise:

Acoustic Guitar

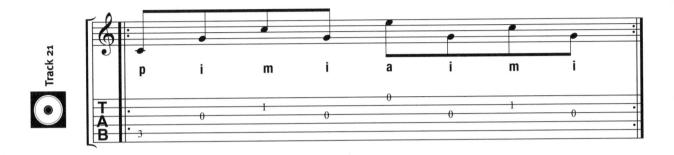

There's nothing too different about it, but you'll have to keep a very watchful eye on things to make sure that this new order is absolutely ship-shape. Work it out from the tab and then listen to the example on the CD. (It's best to check this way if you're at all unsure because practising something incorrectly can be problematic later on. It takes ages to iron those wrinkles out once they're established.) Now here's another variation:

Once again, it's nothing too radical, but it will take effort to get those fingers marching in a different order, so take care.

DAY 24 STUDY

Now that the basic idea of fingerstyle playing is hopefully beginning to establish itself, it's time to play a chord arrangement using this new technique all the way through. This is the type of thing you'll encounter when playing through a

Acoustic Guitar

complete song, and it can be very effective and beautiful, bringing out the very best in guitar accompaniment:

Right-hand fingering is the same throughout

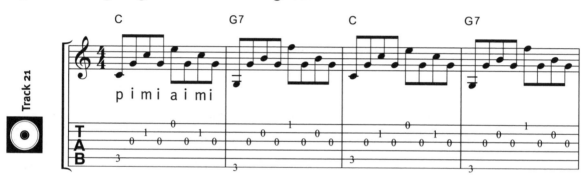

I'm sure I don't have to state the rules again, but your main watchwords here are *slow*, *slow* and *slow*!

DAY 25: ECONOMY OF MOVEMENT

We really have covered a great deal of ground here at quite a speed. Playing a full fingerstyle example like the one we met yesterday after only a couple of days' preparation is quite something, so don't be worried if you're not playing it quite right at this point. Remember that the effects of everything we're covering here are cumulative and you'll have to spend a lot of time on the practice workbench before the clockwork of the situation really begins to run seamlessly.

PRACTICAL EXERCISE

Today we're going to look at a couple of ideas for refining your overall right-hand technique. If you studied the picture of right-hand position a few pages ago, you should be able to see how the fingers sit on the strings on their tips, with the wrist gently arched – a good, tension-free environment that will allow a great deal of movement without undue strain. But let's look even closer at the fingers and consider the actual stroke that sounds the string itself.

If you think about it, each finger has to make a round trip when it strikes a string. It plucks the string by moving inward towards the palm and then drops back, ready to pluck it again another time, so the complete journey it makes is forward to the palm and back to a 'ready to play' position. If you're making this movement correctly, you should really be putting muscular effort only into the first part of the movement; the second should happen automatically and by itself.

EXAMPLES

Try this little experiment: put the guitar down (I realise that you'd hardly be holding it while reading this bit, but I just wanted to make it absolutely clear that this particular exercise doesn't require you to have a guitar in you hands), let your right arm flop down by your side and then bend it at the elbow so that your fingers come up to approximately the level at which you'd strike the strings if the

Acoustic Guitar

guitar was there. Now, imagine that you're pulling the trigger of a gun (for all you pacifists out there who think it's a little brutal to make this kind of suggestion for something as obviously peaceful and benign as playing the guitar, imagine it's a water pistol.) What should happen is that the finger should move back towards the base of the thumb at your command but then spring back by itself. You don't actually have to push it back into position, do you?

This is precisely the movement we're after for plucking the strings. The actual pluck happens when you tell the finger to move, but the return to position happens involuntarily. It's possible only when the hand is in the correct position and there is no tension present. Otherwise it's like pouring grit into an otherwise perfectly serviced machine.

DAY 25 STUDY

Try today's economical-movement idea on a few single notes, like these:

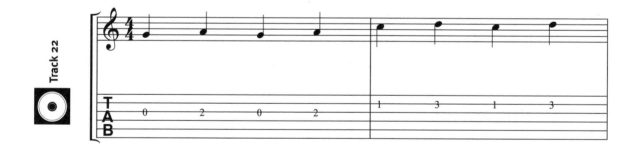

Meanwhile, you should be trying to make sure that yesterday's study piece is progressing nicely. Aim for the absolute minimum hesitation at the chord changes; if the changes are still rough, you're playing the piece too fast and should slow things down again. Remember that getting things smooth and solid at this point will really help you out later on. Remember: you can't speed up a broken machine, so keep yours on the practice workbench until you're sure it's fixed!

Acoustic Guitar

DAY 26: FINGERSTYLE ECONOMY

Playing chords fingerstyle is all very well, but it's really only half the story. Music is made up from three basic elements: harmony, melody and rhythm. What we've covered so far in our look at fingerstyle covers two of these three areas, harmony and rhythm, so what we'll do now is take a look at the vital area of melody playing.

It's often said that, if we could have the best of both worlds, we'd play arpeggios with our fingers (because it's easier than using a plectrum) and melody lines with a pick (because it's easier than using our fingers). But, as I'm sure you don't need me to remind you, the best solution isn't always the most practical, and so we make do with a compromise. (I should mention at this point that such things as fingerpicks and thumbpicks do exists to try to solve this problem, but comparatively few people make them work. You're welcome to try, of course, but I would suggest that you leave this kind of experimentation until your technique is a little more rounded and steady. For now, we'll seek alternatives.)

PRACTICAL EXERCISE

I mentioned earlier that, on steel-string guitar, there isn't a standard way of playing individual notes (ie scale passages or melodies in general) with the right-hand fingers. On classical guitar, there's pretty much a cast-iron tradition, but steel-string players tend to use whichever finger is handy at the time. Of course, this kind of randomness isn't particularly helpful, especially when you're trying to teach fingerstyle, and so I believe that we can learn a little from our classical brethren to the extent that a little bit of discipline doesn't do anyone any harm.

EXAMPLES

The first example here takes the form of an experiment designed to get the basic finger movement started. It's another of those exercises that take place on an open string, so you don't have to keep an eye on what's happening due west.

Acoustic Guitar

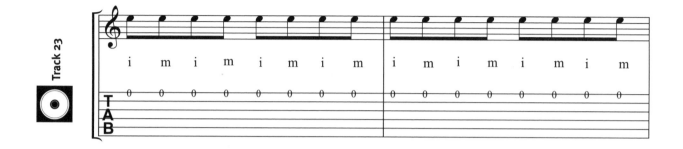

For this, you'll need only the index and middle fingers of the right hand. The idea is that you alternate them like this:

i   m   i   m   i   m   i   m (etc)

Remember that *i* represents your index finger and *m* is your middle finger, so the movement is rather like walking with your fingers, in some ways, but at the same time it's a good way of getting the fingers used to playing individual notes.

Now try this:

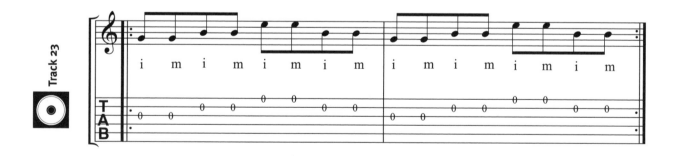

All that's happening here is that you're playing on all three of the top strings of the guitar in the same way as before. There's still nothing happening with your left hand, so full attention can be paid to the left.

Acoustic Guitar

DAY 26 STUDY

In order to really push this idea home, as far as the right hand is concerned, here's another of those 'tongue-twister' exercises for you to look at once you've got the basic idea up and running. This should keep you on your toes, because you're changing strings quite a lot of the time. Aim to achieve a good clean note each time and remember that, if things sound at all blurred, the chances are you're trying to play it too fast. Slow down, be patient and make sure everything else you've studied so far gets its appointed time on your practice workbench.

Track 23

Acoustic Guitar

DAY 27: TREBLE AND BASS

The next step after yesterday's melody-playing trial run is to put everything to good use and play a little tune. This should achieve a couple of things at the same time: firstly, you'll be playing with your fingers and thumb simultaneously; and secondly, you'll be reading something very similar to the type of thing you'll meet out there in the real world. It's challenging, but the chances are you're ready for it.

PRACTICAL EXERCISE

Just before we get into the tune itself, let's just take a look at how the thumb works in all this. As I said, the thumb generally looks after the bass strings – the low E, A and D – while the fingers see to the top three – the G, B and top E. In music, melody is usually supported by either chords, a bassline, or both, so if we're going to play a tune, we'd better make sure our thumbs are up to the task of playing a little bass.

EXAMPLES

Take a look at the following example:

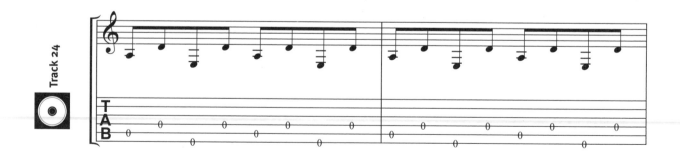

It doesn't look too awkward, does it? But you might find that you need to give the thumb time to find its way between the strings. In the end, you'll be performing

this kind of multitasking with your right hand without thinking about it, but for now you'll probably need to keep looking from hand to page and back again, and things can become quite confusing. If it looks like things are going to descend into chaos at any moment, remember that verbalising the task will often help – that is, with something like this, saying the names of the strings out loud will often straighten out the thumb's tendency to roam onto the wrong string at the wrong moment. The next thing to do is to bring in the fingers. This next exercise involves the thumb and fingers playing together – still on open strings, steering clear of any problems on the fretboard.

Another thing that's happening here is that the thumb is keeping a kind of beat going, and so we're addressing those three musical areas – melody, harmony and rhythm – all at once.

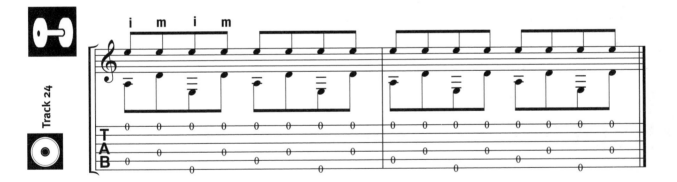

Now we'll move on and involve the left hand:

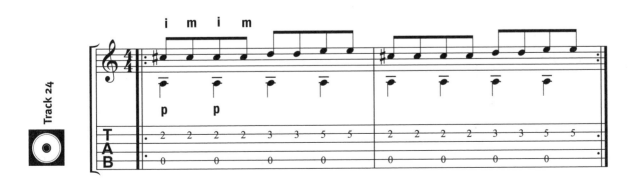

131

Acoustic Guitar

Don't worry if things are beginning to look complex – music always looks difficult on paper. There's a lovely story about a famous jazz musician playing in a club. After he'd finished his set, a member of the audience approached him clutching a piece of manuscript paper (that's what we call the paper music is written down on) and saying, 'Look, I wrote down the solo you played over that last number.' The jazz musician looked at it and said, 'Man, I couldn't play that. It looks way too difficult!'

If you've any doubts, remember that you can always check out what's happening on the CD. I've played all the exercises slowly so that you have the best possible chance of being able to hear what's going on.

DAY 27 STUDY

Today's study piece is another variation on what we've been looking at. It's exactly the same melody, but this time the thumb is moving from the fifth string to the sixth, playing different bass notes:

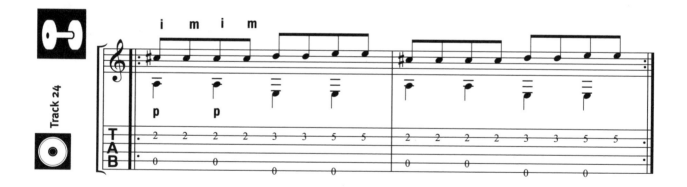

The thumb is still playing on open strings, so there are no worryingly awkward fingering moments to contend with.

Whatever you do, be sure to make the most of these exercises and study pieces and don't let them slip from your practice routine until they're note-perfect and fully up to speed. Even then, it's a good idea to come back to everything you've

learned from Day 1 from time to time and review it. As your overall technique improves, you'll find that you can draw extra benefit from constantly reviewing the very basics – and you'll be strengthening the foundations of your playing when you do.

Acoustic Guitar

DAY 28

WEEK 4 TEST

Another quick quiz to test your mettle in the realm of playing fingerstyle. No starting on Week 5 until you can ace it.

1   What are the four letters that represent the fingering for the right hand?

2   In general, which right-hand fingers are assigned to which strings?

3   Why do guitarists usually have longer nails on their right-hand fingers than their left?

4   Which of the two movements of the plucking fingers should be involuntary?

5   Melody notes tend to be played by alternating which two fingers on the right hand?

6   What are the three basic elements that make music work?

Acoustic Guitar

7   A melody can be supported by chords and what else?

8   Written music always looks more complex than it actually is – true or false?

9   Acknowledging the fingering letters we use for fingerstyle, tap out the word
    'Miami' with your right-hand fingers.

10 Using the same kind of thinking, tap out 'I'm Pam; I'm a mam'.

WEEK 5

Hopefully, the foundations of a good fingerstyle technique have by now been firmly dug in, so you can progress onto pastures newer, if not greener. This week, we'll be looking at a number of areas that will enhance the skills you've already learned, as well as some new techniques. For instance, over the next seven days, we'll be looking at the following:

- Building up your chord repertoire;

- Learning about muting;

- Learning some more arpeggios;

- Making use of the left-hand little finger.

DAY 29: MORE CHORDS!

As before, we'll leave last week's look at basic fingerstyle technique on the back burner while we get on with something else. This constant change is essential to give you the correct amount of time to assimilate into your playing all the various elements we've looked at so far. If you were building a house, you wouldn't expect to spend all your time laying bricks – there's plumbing, electrical work, roofing, carpentry,

QUOTE FOR THE DAY

The first guitar I got was a Spanish guitar. I borrowed it from a friend and never gave it back! – *David Gilmour*

painting and all sorts of other little jobs that all count towards one thing. You only really see the fruits of your labour when you stand back and see the thing you're building beginning to take shape, and that's exactly what we've been doing so far.

PRACTICAL EXERCISE

By now, your chord-playing activities ought to be sounding quite slick. You've had the time to polish the chord exercises for a few days, so now it's time to take this side of your playing a little further.

Let's start by introducing the weakest member of the left hand's troupe of players: the little finger. To begin with, let's look again at the C major chord:

C major

137

Acoustic Guitar

Hopefully the third-finger stretch is beginning to feel more natural now as the hand becomes more accustomed to the task of guitar playing. Now, the first four-finger chord I'm going to introduce to you is based upon this shape, and it goes under the name C7:

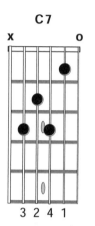

Your fourth (ie little) finger takes its place on the third string, third fret, and you play the top five strings, as before.

At this point, it's a good exercise to play both chords one after the other and try to hear the difference between them. Remember that an awful lot of a guitarist's sense of music comes from training his or her ears – literally introducing those organs to the language of music. And, while we're not overly concerned with some of music's dark and dusty theoretical quarters, learning to hear the difference between two similar chord shapes is still a very positive task.

!

|C maj / / / | C7 / / / | C maj / / / | C7 / / / | C maj / / / | C7 / / / |

It's also a good game of push-ups for the little finger.

Acoustic Guitar

The next item on the list of things to do is introducing yourself to a few more chords. Once again, I fully realise that all these new shapes and names can seem quite bewildering, especially in view of the fact that everything we've been doing over the past weeks has been new to you as well, but realistically all you have to do is play through each of these new chords a couple of times a day, applying the same old checklist if you come across any that give you trouble. You'll soon begin to remember their names – after all, you'll be using them a lot in the future.

D major

E major

A major

D minor

A minor

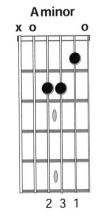

D7

Acoustic Guitar

Of course, strumming a chord is all very well, but we know by now that it's only one way of playing it. So, for today's study (and keeping up my principle of hammering home new information!), here's what your new chords look like when played as arpeggios.

Track 25

Acoustic Guitar

Play through each of the examples a few times so that your fingers get the chance to get the feel of them. Remember that you'll spend an awful lot of time playing chords as a guitar player, so investing a little time here in basic orienteering here is vital.

Acoustic Guitar

DAY 30: THE SEVENTH SIGN, GALLOPING MAJORS AND THE MINORS' STRIKE!

Today, we're going to look at the differences between the chord families that exist in music. Although understanding the basic principles at work here take us dangerously near that minefield known as music theory, it's all essential information and could just save you a lot of time later on when the whole *vive la différence* issue becomes more apparent.

PRACTICAL EXERCISE

In music, there are essentially three chordal families: the majors, the minors and the sevenths. All three are in everyday use, and you can be certain that you'll be spending a lot of time in each others' company, so it's probably best that you become acquainted now.

I'm not going to go into the mechanics of why major chords are different from minors and so on; that really would be too labour-intensive at this stage. A little later on, you might feel inclined to look under music's surface and examine the differences in more detail, but for now it's sufficient to be made aware that such differences do exist – and that they are very important.

EXAMPLES

Take a look at the three chords at the top of the next page:

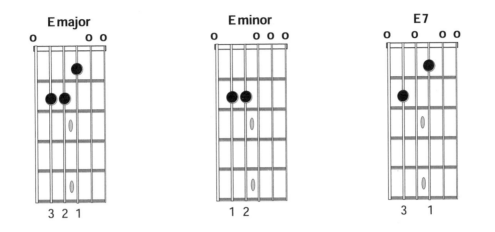

Here we have an E major, an E minor and an E7 chord all lined up for your perusal. What I want you to do is play each of them in turn, one after the other, and listen very carefully to the sound each of them makes. It always helps if you can categorise this sort of thing in some way that's meaningful to you – for instance, when I hear the E major chord, to me it sounds full and positive and very sure of itself, while the E minor sounds sad and slightly unsure, quite a contrast from the major version. The seventh, meanwhile, sounds somehow inconclusive and incomplete, as if it wants to go somewhere else, which is why I always think of seventh chords as being a little like commas – you wouldn't use them to conclude something, because they don't sound quite finished. (In fact there's a whole cartful of music theory that backs up this opinion, but I won't bore you with it here!)

Whatever your own individual analysis with regard to how these different chords sound to you, the most vital thing to grasp is that they are all essentially different, despite the fact that they share the common root of E. So, when you see an E7 chord called for, playing an E minor instead simply won't do; the differences between them are there for a reason, and so it's best to make sure that you keep everything you play in the right family, chordally speaking.

Acoustic Guitar

In today's study, we have some more chords lined up in their family groups. All I want you to do is play each of them through, one after the other, and try to hear their different family characteristics. Oh, and just to make things even more interesting, I've written them out as arpeggios, just to keep that right hand of yours on its toes!

Track 26

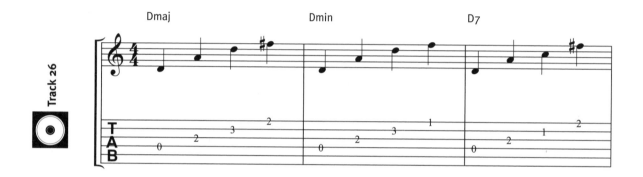

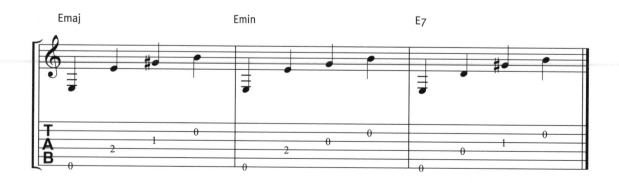

DAY 31: THE UGLY BUNCH

It has to be said that on the guitar there are easy chords, more difficult chords
and some real stinkers! Today, I'm going to introduce you to the members of the
various chord families that spend most of their time locked in the attic...

PRACTICAL EXERCISE

So far, we've looked at one-finger, two-finger, three-finger and four-finger chords,
and you might be thinking that there aren't really any more digital variations
available to us. But you'd be wrong.

Given the fact that we haven't got any more fingers to use on the fretboard, our
only real choice is to use one finger to cover two strings. This isn't something that
happens all the time, I'll grant you, but there are some chords in very common use
that depend on a little bit of digital agility on your behalf to make them work.

EXAMPLES

Let's look at exhibit A in this house of horrors:

F major

This is the F chord – aptly named, I think you'll agree! Before you try playing it
from cold and hurt yourself, however, you'd do well to read this next bit.

Acoustic Guitar

Earlier, I mentioned how our general anatomy has to adapt to the stresses and strains that guitar playing places upon it, and the chord of F major is a very good example of this in action. The index finger has to lay itself over both the E and B strings while the second and third fingers take up their positions on the G and D strings respectively. If you've already tried this particular chord, you're not the first to believe it's impossible and that you'll never get your fingers around it, but one of the most important elements in getting around this is time; your index finger has to adapt and gain some flexibility in the joint at its tip before the chord will feel at all natural.

Now, the good thing is that this is almost guaranteed to occur eventually; the bad news is that it will continue to slow you down in the meantime. It's frustrating, I know, but just trust me – you'll look back on all this one day and laugh heartily.

While we're on the subject of the chord-book bogeymen, let's look at a couple of other shapes that take that little extra bit of finger choreography to get dead right:

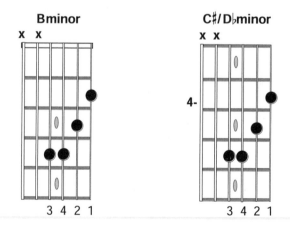

You aren't expected to hold down more than one string per finger this time, but somehow these minor chords are far from straightforward in execution. Once again, all I'm inviting you to do here is familiarise yourself with these shapes and

keep them turning over on the practice workbench. They'll become easier and easier with time, *but only if they're worked upon regularly.* Many guitarists try to deal with the instrument's more difficult moments by ignoring them and hoping they'll go away, but they won't; I've known plenty of students who hid under the bedclothes rather than confront some of the guitar's tiny terrors, but things didn't improve by themselves.

DAY 31 STUDY

If you thought that the F chord was bad, just wait until we start talking about barre chords (sometimes spelled *bar*, although I prefer the original spelling because I'm hopelessly pedantic). Barre chords involve one finger holding down all six strings on the fretboard before any other fingers are laid down to form a chord. Mission impossible? Well, maybe at present, but we can begin some of the basic spadework necessary to make barre chords a bit easier when we have to involve them in our playing.

So, today's study piece is a bit of a puzzle for you. First of all, I want you to place your index finger over three strings, as shown in this handy diagram:

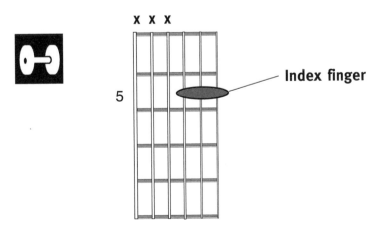

That's all – don't do anything else quite yet. Now check your thumb position at the back of the neck and make sure that it's in a suitably supportive position. It

Acoustic Guitar

ought to look as if you're just about to pinch something (or someone) between your index finger and thumb, if you weren't holding a guitar neck. One other thing to check would be to make sure that the first finger is locked in position behind the fret and stopping off the strings efficiently.

Next, try to play each of the three strings in turn, one at a time, and see if you have a clean note. If so, then bravo! Tell yourself that you're a natural and get on with the rest of your practice routine. If not, just run through the checklist, make some refining movements with the left hand, keep an eye on the thumb position and keep trying until you get a full complement of notes each time. There's probably only one way of playing this particular exercise accurately, and most of us have found it by this kind of trial-and-error approach, so don't be downhearted if, once again, you can't seem to get the knack immediately. Keep reviewing it in your practice time and things will begin to work eventually.

DAY 32: CHORD ARRANGEMENTS (PART I)

Today we're going to look at some familiar chord arrangements of the type that you'll be meeting when you start playing songs. One of the more convenient factors that music offers up is that similar chord arrangements crop up time and time again, so with a little experience you'll soon find that there are fewer and fewer things around to phase you.

One of the most common chord arrangements in popular music (I use this term to cover everything that isn't classical music; don't worry, I'm not accusing you of wanting to play pop) is a blues. Now, I'd understand absolutely if you were to tell me that you didn't want to play the blues, and I'm not going to suggest for one second that this is the direction we're going to take. What I'm drawing your attention to is the influence that this particular music form has had throughout contemporary music's history.

Today, of course, the blues style is still around – a very modern version of it, to be sure, but one that remains true to its roots – and the imprint it has left on guitar playing in particular is evident in practically all forms of music.

EXAMPLES

One of the more obvious thumbprints that blues has left on modern music is in its chord arrangement. Arguably, one of the most common chord arrangements in rock or pop music would be something called a *12-bar-blues*, which takes its name from the fact that it's based around a 12-bar pattern that repeats for the full length of the song. This is unusual in music, because most songs have a chorus, but blues songs tend not to.

So let's look at a stripped-down version of the 12-bar blues:

Acoustic Guitar

Track 27

A7 / / /	A7 / / /	A7 / / /	A7 / / /
D7 / / /	D7 / / /	A7 / / /	A7 / / /
E7 / / /	D7 / / /	A7 / / /	A7 / / /	

Here's a reminder of the chords we'll be using:

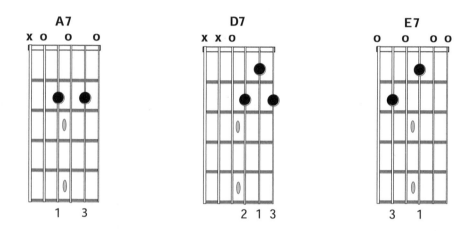

If chord changes still tend to hold things up, play through each of them and make a note of what sort of finger movements (in the air, remember, not on the neck) are necessary to change between chords.

In order to play this example, you'll have to change between A7 and D7 first of all. Look at the differences between these two shapes, experiment with them on the neck and look hard at exactly what the left hand has to do to make the transition. Then do the same for the A7–E7 and E7–D7 changes.

This sort of preparation is good because it ensures that the chord changes won't sound foreign to you this way around. We're aiming for smooth chord changes and a tempo that doesn't falter, so isolating any potential problem areas beforehand and dealing with them makes perfect sense.

Play through the chord arrangement at an easy, slow tempo, using four downstrokes of the plectrum per bar and speeding up only when you're absolutely sure that all of the changes are perfectly glitch-free.

DAY 32 STUDY

One variation on today's chord arrangement for a 12-bar blues crops up quite regularly, and so I thought it would make a good study. Known to the trade as a *quick-change blues*, it involves an extra change between the A7 and D7 chords, breaking up that initial four bars of A7, which can get deadly dull and repetitious, especially at slower tempos.

```
| A7 / / / | D7 / / / | A7 / / / | A7 / / / |
| D7 / / / | D7 / / / | A7 / / / | A7 / / / |
| E7 / / / | D7 / / / | A7 / / / | A7 / / / ||
```

Remember to watch out for those 'x' markings on the chord boxes; the A7 is a five-string chord, the E7 uses all six strings, but the D7 employs the top four only. Any accidental bass notes ringing out in the wrong place will make everything sound confused and, quite frankly, wrong.

Acoustic Guitar

DAY 33: CHORD ARRANGEMENTS (PART II)

In this lesson, we'll take a look at another common chord arrangement and learn a new technique called *muting*.

It would be impossible for us to look at all the variations of chord arrangements available in modern music. There are literally hundreds of different arrangements out there and a great many different ways of playing each. Throw in a few more variations like tempo and style (ie reggae or rock – there could be a common chord arrangement between two songs, but the differences between styles would make them sound very different to each other) and you're looking at considerably more. So we'll content ourselves for now with looking at just a few in order to prepare the way for later on.

Take a look at the chord arrangement below:

Track 28

Dmaj / / /	Gmaj / / /	A7 / / /	Dmaj / / /
Gmaj / / /	Gmaj / / /	Dmaj / / /	Dmaj / / /
Gmaj / / /	Gmaj / / /	Dmaj / / /	Dmaj / / /
A7 / / /	A7 / / /	Dmaj / / /	Dmaj / / /	

Once again, you're dealing with only three chords. Here they are as a reminder:

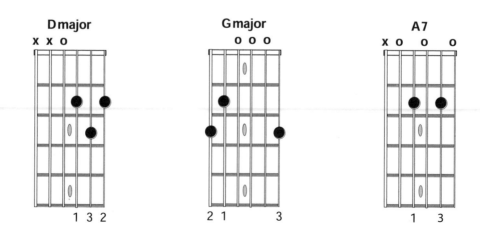

If you apply the same kind of preparation work to this arrangement as we did with the blues, you'll find that things run much smoother, so spend a few minutes considering what has to happen when you change between the D, A and G chords before you tackle them all *in situ*.

As far as our newly learned muting technique is concerned, you can use it here to control the unwanted ringing-on of strings from chord to chord, and a lot more besides – for instance, it's possible to make a chord accompaniment sound much more punchy by using some right-hand muting, so let's look at how it's done.

EXAMPLES

Let's begin with another experiment. First of all, I want you to sound all of your open strings with a single strum of either fingers or pick. Now lay your picking hand down on the strings and cut off the ringing completely. (There's an example of this on Track 28 of the CD if you have any problems.) Basically, we're using the edge of the right-hand palm as a damper to control how long a chord lasts. The sound of chords ringing into each other has one set of characteristics, while some judicious muting will change things quite radically.

This is another one of those techniques that will take a bit of time to blend into your playing. In practice, it's one of those discretionary techniques that players use to help sculpt the sound they're making, but for now it's a good idea to become acquainted with it and work with it a little as an investment for later on.

At first, it's awkward to perform the triple tasks of holding a pick, strumming and muting all at once, but you'll find later on that these actions combine together into a single picking movement, controlling the chords you're playing to great effect.

DAY 33 STUDY

Today's study follows on from our look at right-hand muting. It's a little workout that will help you to become accustomed with the bare bones of this important

Acoustic Guitar

technique, which, as I said previously, will come in very handy later on. First of all, let's nominate a chord that you're really familiar with, good old C major:

Track 28

C major

Here's what I want you to do. Play the chord with either your plectrum or fingers; hit it quite hard and listen to the sustain and decay. (It should go on for around nine or ten seconds under normal domestic acoustic conditions.) Now hit the chord again, but count to three and gently lay the fleshy edge of your right hand palm-down on the strings just in front of the bridge and cut the sound off. (Be careful not to be too enthusiastic, or you'll be able to hear a slap as you mute, which ought to be avoided.)

Now do exactly the same thing, this time counting to two and then one. Finally, cut off the chord immediately after having played it to produce a highly accented stab. Repeat this exercise a number of times (and bring it out onto the practice workbench every so often to review it) until you're really comfortable with the movements involved.

Acoustic Guitar

DAY 34: CHORD ARRANGEMENTS (PART III)

Today we'll look at another chord arrangement – slightly more difficult than before, but even more like the ones you'll encounter when you start to work through songbooks.

Here's today's chord chart:

Track 29

Cmaj / Amin /	Fmaj / Gmaj /
Cmaj / Amin /	Fmaj / Gmaj /
Cmaj / / /	C7 / / /	Fmaj / / /	Fmin / / /
Cmaj / Amin /	Fmaj / G7 /	Cmaj	

To begin with, you'll notice that I've included the nightmare F major chord (plus one that you don't know yet) in the interests of making this as 'real' as possible. When you start working through songbooks, you're going to find awkward chords stuck in the middle of song arrangements, and you're going to have to deal with them accordingly. (As I've said before, please don't do what so many people do and ignore all the songs with bogeyman chords in them or you'll never be able to deal with them when you have to!) Once you've gained a little experience in meeting the awkward along with the easy, you'll soon learn to wade in and make the best of things.

EXAMPLES

It's often the case in real life that, every so often, you meet chords that you don't yet know. An important addition to your library at this point, therefore, would be a good chord book – as long as you promise me that you won't use it like a tutor by trying to learn every chord, but more like a dictionary. Refer to it to look up chords as and when you need them, and keep it in your guitar case or on your bookshelf at all other times.

Acoustic Guitar

So here's the F minor chord for you to take a look at:

F minor

x x

3 1 1 1

Now, I know what you're thinking at this point: 'Do I have to put my first finger over all three top strings and put my third finger in there somewhere too?' Well, yes, you do. Sorry.

In my defence, I did get you to do a little preparation for this a few days ago, so it shouldn't come as a huge shock to the system. You probably won't need me to tell you that you'll find this exercise very awkward to play initially – but I hope that you also won't need me to tell you that practising it on the workbench will make it easier and easier, given a fair amount of patience and time.

If all that wasn't bad enough, I've also engineered things so that you're playing chords for only two beats per bar a lot of the time. This actually works in quite a logical way. Take a look at these two chords:

| Cmaj / Fmaj / |

In the example above, you would count 'one, two' on the C chord and 'three, four' on the F. This situation will probably be new to you, so you can expect it to be unfamiliar and cause a few bumps in the road at first, but deal with it the same

Acoustic Guitar

way as you would other problems: take it out of your exercise routine and practise it in isolation a few times first, replacing it only when you're confident that it won't cause too much of a problem when played *in situ*.

This is, without doubt, the most challenging chord chart you've encountered so far, but it's also the most realistic, so working away at this will undoubtedly prepare you for what you'll find Out There.

DAY 34 STUDY

In order to prepare you even more for the forthcoming horror of barre chords (we looked at these a little a couple of days ago, I know) I want you to go one more step. The F minor chord in today's lesson is part of a group known as *part-barre chords* (as opposed to *full-barre chords*). They're challenging, frustrating and awkward, but they're also essential to your playing.

Seeing as there's a lot of muscular development that's got to happen before this type of chord starts to feel easier, you'll forgive me if I keep cracking away at them and getting you to perform ever more ghastly contortions with your left hand, but, as every grandmother on Earth has said at least once, it's doing you good. Today's variation involves holding down the full barre in the middle of the guitar neck (it's easier up here than it is down at the nut) and placing your third finger on the fifth string to form a chord known as a *minor seventh*.

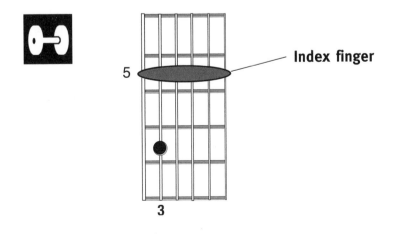

Index finger

5

3

Acoustic Guitar

I don't expect immediate results from this, and neither should you. It's merely something else to include in your daily routine so that it begins to feel natural after a while. Take care with it and don't carry on practising if it begins to hurt or cramp your hand. Your body is understandably going to put up a bit of resistance to all this unnatural stuff you're asking it to do, but if you're patient and persistent, it will ultimately oblige.

DAY 35

WEEK 5 TEST

Yes, you guessed it – another dastardly exposé of you knowledge (or lack thereof) of the techniques covered in the previous chapter. No cheating now...

1   What are the three chord families known as?

2   Think of a word that sums up the sound of a minor chord.

3   Which two strings does the left-hand first finger have to hold down to form an F major chord?

4   Why is thumb position vitally important when playing barre chords?

5   What is one of the 12-bar blues's more non-conformist traits?

6   Why do we need to use muting?

Acoustic Guitar

7 What's the best way to use a chord book?

8 What name is given to chords that require you to place your first finger halfway across the fingerboard?

9 Which punctuation mark best sums up the sound of a seventh chord?

10 How do you count a bar with different chords on the first and last two beats?

WEEK 6

This week we'll be learning about rhythm, one of the essential ingredients in your playing. Without a sense of rhythm, music becomes lifeless and flaccid, but a good, strong sense of rhythm will help to focus your playing and make it come alive. Here's a brief breakdown of what we'll be looking at:

- Quarter note, eighth note and 16th-note rhythm;

- How to count through a song;

- Alternate strumming and picking;

- Different time signatures;

- Volume and tone.

DAY 36: I GOT RHYTHM

Cast your mind back a few days to when I told you about the three basic elements that make up music. I said that it was basically a mix of harmony (which we've looked at in the form of chords), melody (which we've looked at in learning to play melody notes and will be coming back to next week) and rhythm (which is sort of limping along, trying to join in when it can).

QUOTE FOR THE DAY

Everybody in my street had a guitar and all we did was listen to the radio and steal everything we could from there.
— *Robert Cray*

PRACTICAL EXERCISE

So far, we've experimented with down- and upstrokes and seen the differences that exist between them. However, in order to become fully fledged purveyors of rhythm, we need to delve further into the inner workings of guitar music and see what sort of thing goes on. The following exercise should give you some idea of what's involved.

At its most basic, our rhythm playing so far has been structured around this kind of pattern:

| Cmaj / / / |

Here, there's no real rhythmic direction at all, other than the fact that we have to play a C major chord four times – or, rather, for four beats. The actual style and type of rhythm hasn't been specified, and so – as quite often happens – it's left up to us. I guess you could say that rhythmic style is, for the most part, discretionary...

EXAMPLES

So how exactly do we go about bringing a little rhythmic variety into the average chord pattern? To understand a little more about how this rhythm business works, we'll have to sneak a look under the covers of music theory. Don't worry, we won't be venturing too far, just enough to get the general idea.

Practically all music has some kind of a beat. It's this that makes you want to tap your foot, or even dance if you're that way inclined (and here I must admit that I'm not – no amount of cajoling, threats, friendly persuasion or even alcohol has been known to get me onto the dance floor; I'm one of nature's wallflowers). So, given that most Western music has a sort of natural rhythm to it in the form of a beat, this is usually split up into bite-sized chunks of equal length called *bars* – which we met earlier in our look at chord charts.

By far the most common sort of rhythm is known as 4/4, which means that there are four beats to the bar – exactly as we've been playing so far, in fact. (4/4 is known as a *time signature* in music parlance. Just thought you'd like to know!) But a beat can be divided up into smaller units, meaning that we can have four beats to the bar but eight 'strums', as shown here:

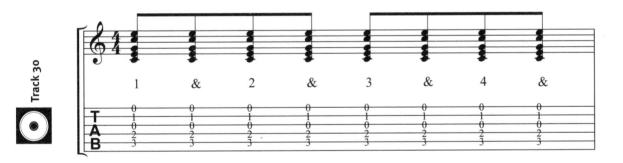

If your picking skills have developed accordingly, it's even possible (and not at all unusual, especially in rock circles) to have 16 pick movements per bar:

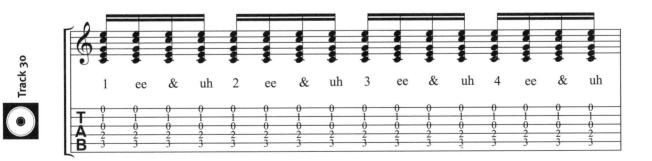

163

Acoustic Guitar

The most important thing here is that the rhythm is still *felt* as being in groups of four and not obscured or confused by the pattern your right hand chooses to play.

Now let's make a practical exercise out of these mathematical beat divisions and see how each of them works. So far, we've been treating a bar like this one as comprising four downstrokes…

| Cmaj / / / |

…and there's absolutely nothing wrong with doing it that way. Dividing the beat in half would mean that we'd have to play the C chord eight times in the bar, and as we've seen before, this is best performed with alternating up- and downstrokes:

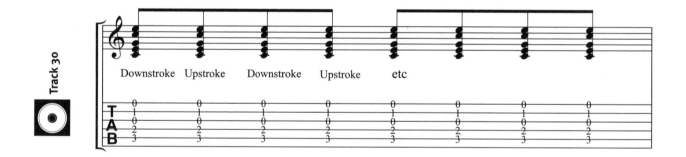

The weight on the first half of each beat helps the ear to pinpoint that all-important beat, and later on you'll find that a little right-hand muting can help to shape things even more.

Of course, there's nothing to stop you from playing eight downstrokes, if that's what suits the particular song you're playing.

Acoustic Guitar

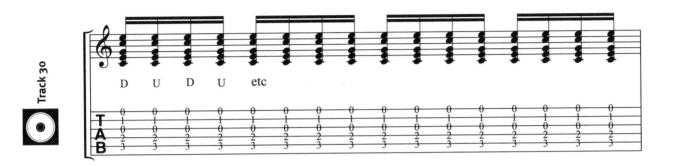

D   U   D   U   etc

Play the two examples to compare them (and listen to the way I've played them on the CD) and you'll be able to hear the difference. In order to play the rarer 16th-note rhythm, you might find that some players deal with this by using downstrokes, as up-and-down strumming at this level of rhythmic intensity can sound really wild and unfocused at anything other than really slow tempos. On the other hand, alternate strumming on funk 16th-note passages is not uncommon.

Muting is almost certainly mandatory here, as otherwise there's much too much unwanted sustain, or 'ringing on', in the strings.

DAY 36 STUDY

In order to put our look at rhythm into some kind of perspective, today's study material focuses on swapping between all three of the basic patterns over the duration of five bars of music, as shown in the figure over the page:

Acoustic Guitar

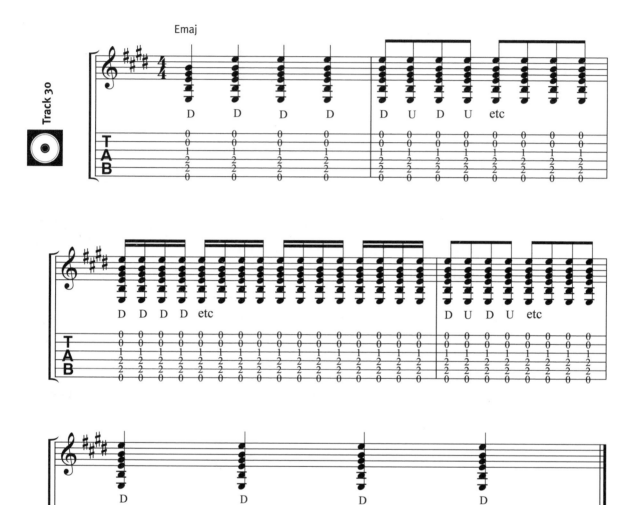

The above material is all based on a single chord, allowing you to focus your attention on your right hand exclusively – and I can guarantee that this one will drive everyone around you mad after only a little while. This really is the unsociable end of learning to play guitar!

DAY 37: BEAUTY AND THE BEAT

Given that we've learned briefly how to accommodate the more common 'beat splits' in a picking routine, don't go thinking that things have to remain this static. You'll probably agree that keeping an eight-to-the-bar rhythm going for the duration of a song will sound a little tired after only a short time, so why not have a crack at varying it a little?

PRACTICAL EXERCISE

This is what I meant about right-hand rhythm on the guitar being largely discretionary. If you listen to a cross-section of acoustic-guitar accompaniment on record, you'll rarely be able to find anything that stays constant throughout any given piece of music. It's usually a mixed bag with the sole purpose of driving the song along. The beat's still very much there, prominent and to the fore, but the acoustic guitar is working around it, filling it out and keeping things focused and interesting at the same time.

EXAMPLES

Yesterday we examined three very basic strumming patterns for the right hand, and so today we'll look at ways of varying things using the tried-and-tested method of mixing and matching. Naturally, you can't afford to be totally random in this respect – and you've always got to pick and choose according to the overall mood of the piece you're accompanying – but even when the concept is reduced to an exercise, you should be able to see the principles involved.

First of all, we're going to learn some verbal patter to help us count through the following exercises. Counting is essential to begin with (and it's still a pretty good idea after that), and you'll soon find that, if you try to tackle rhythm playing without basing your thinking around counting, things can very quickly slip into absolute pandemonium, rhythmically speaking, and you'll learn nothing at all. In

Acoustic Guitar

fact, under the most ideal circumstances, you really need some kind of external tool to help you pace yourself through these kinds of exercises. A metronome is the best thing for the job, but a drum machine or even a loudly ticking clock would do. You just need some sort of external pulse that will keep a beat going relentlessly while you experiment over the top.

For single-beat downward strums, we'll simply count 'one, two, three, four', as shown below:

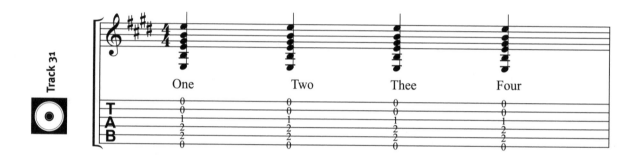

When we split the beat in half, we'll amend this to '*one* and *two* and *three* and *four* and', like this:

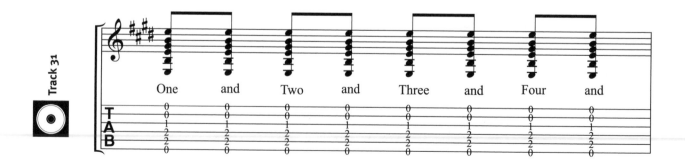

And finally, for the four-on-a-beat variety of up-and-down strumming, we'll count '*one*-e-and-uh *two*-e-and-uh *three*-e-and-uh *four*-e-and-uh', like so:

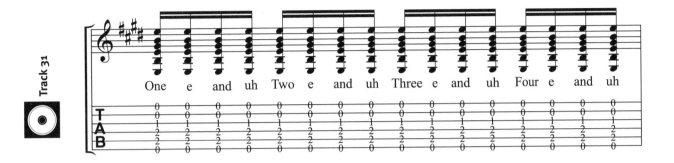

Naturally, anyone within earshot who hears you counting away like this will think you're a little crazy, but you'll probably find that this just adds to the mystique of learning music.

On to the actual exercises, then. We'll start off at a very basic level:

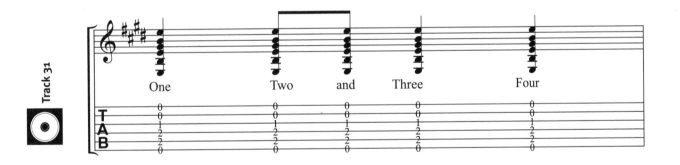

Here, you'd count 'one two-and three four'. If you're at all mystified by the counting, take a listen to the example on the CD and all will be made clear.

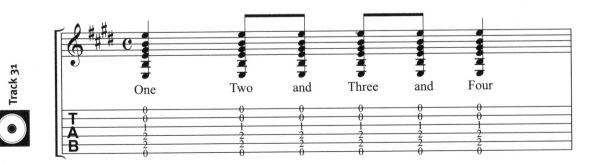

169

Acoustic Guitar

The counting pattern for this exercise is 'one two-and three-and four'. Watch that rhythm, though; the usual mistakes involved here are speeding up, slowing down and not bisecting those beats correctly.

Today's study follows on from the day's lesson. Here I've constructed four more rhythms for you to play – but this time I'm not going to work out the counting regime for you. I want you to write it out yourself in light pencil over the top of each exercise and then – *and only then* – check the CD to make sure you were right.

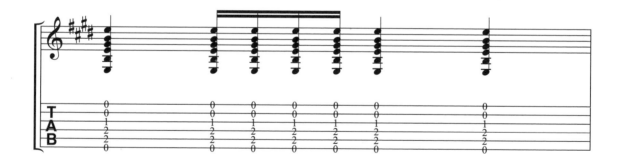

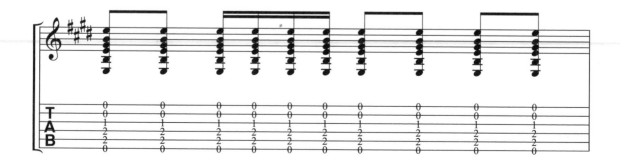

170

Acoustic Guitar

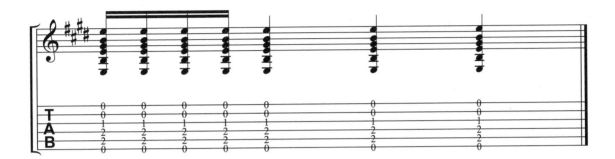

Counting is fundamentally important in music. In future, you'll find that working out some form of verbal patter – phrases that suit the rhythms you're trying to play – will help you to solve the rhythmic riddles you come across on a daily basis.

Acoustic Guitar

DAY 38: MORE RHYTHMIC VARIATIONS

So far, we've met with only the most common rhythmic format in music: 4/4 rhythm. Translated back into plain English, this means that each bar of a given piece comprises four beats, each of which is known as a *quarter note*. You don't need to worry too much about the quarter-note side of the equation just yet, but if you're really interested, a quarter note looks like this…

…and you'll generally find plenty of them in any given piece of music.

PRACTICAL EXERCISE

Occasionally, you're going to find songs that aren't 4/4 – although, as I said, this is by far the most common time signature in music. Today, we'll look at a couple of others in common usage, just so that you're prepared for most things when you venture out alone into the wacky world of songbooks.

EXAMPLES

You've probably heard of waltzes, although you could be forgiven for thinking that you'd never actually take part in one! One of the principal characteristics of a waltz is its time signature, which is traditionally 3/4, as opposed to 4/4. All this means to us, on the face of it, is that instead of a bar of music looking like this…

| Cmaj / / / |

…we get one that looks like this:

| Cmaj / / |

Alternatively, you might find a clue to a piece of music's basic time signature at the beginning of the score, in which case 4/4 looks like this...

...and 3/4 looks like this:

It's even possible that you'll find 2/4, which looks like this...

| Cmaj / |

...or appears as a fraction at the start of the music, like this:

Each time signature is dealt with in exactly the same way, however. Like I said, you'd be advised to adopt some kind of verbal patter that will help you through the piece rhythmically, and try to keep everything as metrically perfect as possible.

Acoustic Guitar

As with yesterday's study session, here are some examples of different time signatures and strumming patterns for you to work through. As before, I want you to try to work out each of them yourself before checking the CD version to make sure you've hit the target.

Use any chord to strum rhythm patterns

Track 32

DAY 39: PICKING IN RHYTHM

So much for strumming chords – and I'll admit that we've only skimmed the surface of the very broad subject of rhythm. But now what about individual notes? How are these best approached?

We've already done a little work on the subject of picking, and we've looked at what happens when we want to play a melody line with our fingers. Now we're going to consider how to discipline those melodic lines rhythmically.

PRACTICAL EXERCISE

To begin with, let's fine-tune our plectrum technique a little. As far as holding the pick is concerned, the default way is to place it between the right hand forefinger and thumb, as shown here:

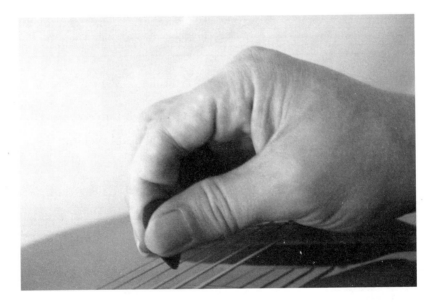

It's really only the top 2–3mm of the pick that's used for playing individual notes

Acoustic Guitar

In general, only the tip of the pick – probably only the first 2–3mm, in fact – is used to strike the strings. If you use any more, or dig deeper with the pick, you'll actually find that you're adversely affecting the sound. If you play chords using too much of the pick, they'll sound brash and ragged, while if you play single notes this way, you'll have to lift the pick too far between each stroke, impairing the fluency of any melody you might be playing.

EXAMPLES

Now let's transfer what we know about basic rhythmic strumming technique over to playing individual notes with a plectrum. In actual fact, much of what we've already learned stays in place. Individual 4/4 beats would therefore most likely be played using consecutive downstrokes, like this...

...whereas eighth notes – ie 'one-and two-and'-type rhythmic configurations – would be made up from alternate 'down-up' picking:

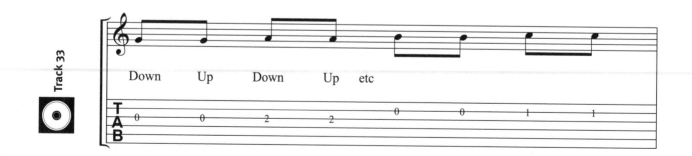

Advancing to 16th-note ('one-e-and-uh') rhythm, we'd find that this alternate-picking strategy stays in place:

This is another important foundation stone in your playing. Alternate picking makes use of both up and down movements of the hand, so nothing is wasted in terms of time and motion. It's an economical and efficient playing style, and hence it's worth taking some time to establish it in your playing at this stage.

I'm not saying, of course, that everything you pick from now on will use this kind of picking regime – once again, picking can be discretionary in many respects – but what I definitely *am* saying is that alternate picking will form the basis of a great deal of the individual lines that you play.

DAY 39 STUDY

Needless to say, following on from the theme we've established this week for study pieces, over the page I've laid out some picking exercises designed specifically to hone the idea of alternate picking down to a fine edge. Everything here is based on open strings – we'll be adding some notes for the left hand to fret later on:

Acoustic Guitar

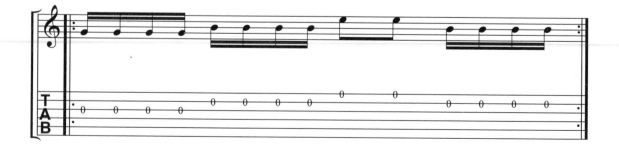

Acoustic Guitar

DAY 40: VOLUME AND TONE

If there's a common fault amongst acoustic players in the early stages of their playing careers, it's not making the best use of the natural dynamics which reside in their instrument. Many players tend to play really quietly – possibly unsure of themselves and naturally a little inhibited – but this really isn't that good for the guitar. It's a fact that guitars sound their best when they're being played at around 70%–80% of their natural dynamic range.

PRACTICAL EXERCISE

Try this test: play absolutely anything you like from any of the exercises we've looked at so far – a chord, maybe, or a series of notes – as quietly as you can. Listen hard to the sound you're making: you don't want it so quiet that there's no tone left in the strings. Thin and reedy-sounding isn't attractive under most circumstances, so if this is the sound you're getting, step on the gas with your plectrum or fingers a little until everything sounds a lot more solid. When you're happy that you've reached the perfect compromise between quiet and sounding good, move on to stage 2...

Now I want you to play the same thing as before, but this time as loud as you can. Once again, you'll notice that, if you put too much energy into the string with your pick or fingers, things will start to sound brash and ugly. If this is the case, back off a little until you reach the balance between volume and good tone.

What you're discovering here is your instrument's natural *dynamic range*, from its quietest voice to its loudest. Dynamics are incredibly important in music – they help give it life and offer contrast in both accompaniment and melody. Repeat this exercise a few times, and keep repeating it every so often in your practice routine so that you can move between these two vital parameters with ease and so that your understanding of loud and soft is constantly under review.

Acoustic Guitar

Your acoustic guitar has a tone control. Arguably, it actually has more than one, but the one we're going to look at here is the easiest to understand immediately. You'll have noticed that the natural position assumed by most players when playing acoustic guitar is with the picking hand either over or just to the right of the soundhole (from a player's perspective, of course). There's not really any particular reason for this, it seems; it's just something everyone seems to fall into.

Try this experiment: take any exercise from the book so far and play it in the position mentioned above, taking careful note of the sound you're making, especially the tonal quality. Now move your picking hand to the left of the soundhole, so that you're playing nearer the guitar's fingerboard, and compare the results. You should find that the sound has mellowed slightly. Perhaps it sounds marginally sweeter? More rounded?

Next, play the exercise or chord shape again, but this time make sure that you pluck or pick the strings directly in front of the guitar's bridge. Take a good listen: you should be able to hear that the sound has become slightly more bright and treble-sounding.

If you play in these the three different positions, one after the other, it should sound a bit like someone turning the tone control up and down on a radio, with the sound moving from sweet and subtle to bright and boisterous just by altering your picking position.

Just as we established the parameters on your guitar relating to volume, we've now marked out the tonal range, too. Even though you might think that subtleties like this should lie further in the future, I've found that it's good to introduce them at a fairly early stage, making players comparatively new to the instrument aware of the facilities available to them. After all, I bet if you'd have bought an electric guitar, you'd have sat fiddling with the volume and tone controls to see what they did!

Acoustic Guitar

Today's study piece is a follow-through from what we were doing yesterday –
except that I'm going to add another dimension to the proceedings by giving you
some notes to play with the left hand, along with a couple of directions as to how
loud or quiet I want you to play and whether I want the tone bright or mellow.

Track 34

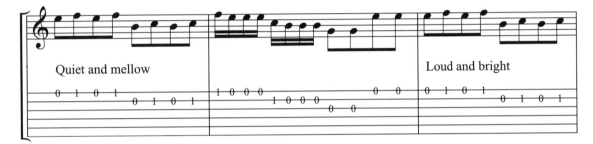

181

DAY 41: FINGERSTYLE RHYTHM

So much for varying your strumming patterns to add interest in an accompaniment. But what about fingerpicking? How does this fit into the rhythm plan?

To begin with, let's agree that rhythm is rhythm – it's a thing that's based in mathematics, to the extent that beats are normally divided and subdivided in accordance with the number of beats in a particular bar. The beat itself is the most important factor here, too; if your listener loses track of where the music's basic rhythmic heartbeat lies, things can get pretty chaotic.

So, no matter whether we're strumming along to a song, playing a melody line or fingerpicking, a little bit of maths has to be done in advance. Of course, musicians don't travel around with pocket calculators, working out exactly what they should be doing over any given beat; most of the time, this sort of thing is felt – it's something that comes from inside. As an example, I'd say that we're all born with an innate sense of rhythm; even very young children will react when they hear music and will often try to move their bodies in time with it. All we have to do as adults – good old self-conscious grown-ups – is to tap into this natural resource and all our rhythmic problems are solved. That's not to say that we won't have to try to wake the sleeping beast first, though...

EXAMPLES

Our look at fingerstyle so far has covered many of the basics involved, the pure fingers-on-strings side of things, but we can't neglect the other important side – rhythm – any longer, so let's try to work out a plan.

We know that, at its very core, the rhythm business depends on splitting beats into two or four (it's also possible to split a beat into three, five or any number you like, but that kind of wizardry goes way beyond the scope of this book), but how can we adapt fingerpicking patterns accordingly? Well, let's begin by looking at that very familiar C major chord:

Acoustic Guitar

C major

If we play it this way, we have four notes:

Now, we know that four is a good figure, from a rhythmic point of view, because it would fit across either two beats or perhaps only one:

Acoustic Guitar

(Incidentally, I know that the previous bit of written music won't make a lot of sense to you, but I'm hoping to stimulate your curiosity a little.) Play the example above and count just as you did with the strumming patterns and you should find that everything fits like a rhythmic glove. But does it *really* fit? What about the return journey? If we merely reverse what we have in the example above, we get this:

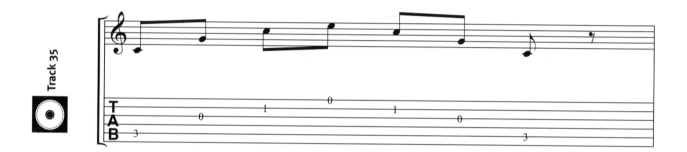

We're one note short, and so we have to adapt the fingerpicking pattern to suit and make sure that it's a perfect fit, like this:

Now we can play the C chord twice in a single bar of 4/4 rhythm without fear of upsetting the apple cart.

Acoustic Guitar

You can now add this all-important dimension of rhythm to your fingerpicking activities, so I guess I'd better come up with some study pieces. These will stand up under any performance circumstance.

With a view to getting the idea of rhythmic fingerpicking really well embedded, here's a couple of other chord-based, metrically correct fingerpicking patterns:

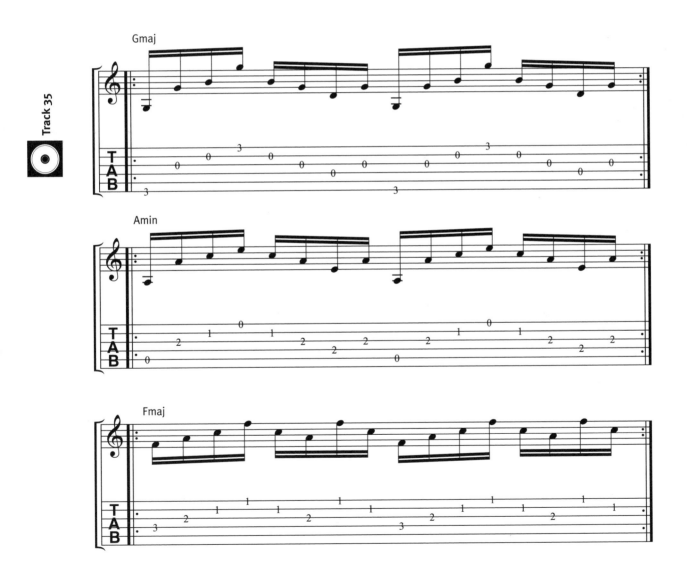

Acoustic Guitar

And now, a fingerpicking exercise for you to practise. Try to ensure that everything works, rhythmically, by either counting or using a metronome. Use the CD track as a guide.

Track 35

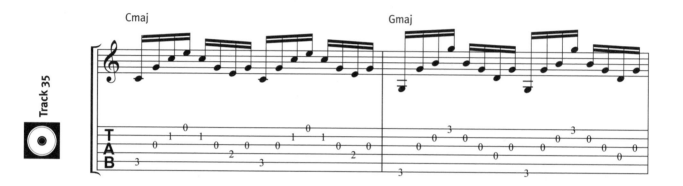

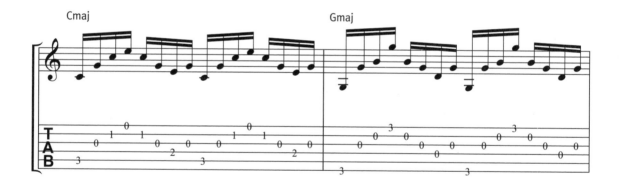

Acoustic Guitar

DAY 42

WEEK 6 TEST

OK, now things are starting to get interesting! Pit your wits against this stinker of a quiz, designed to separate the men from the boys...

1   What's another word for a handy, bite-sized chunk of music?

2   What name is given to the most common rhythm found in music?

3   What time signature would you associate with a waltz?

4   Why does a metronome make such a fabulous birthday present for the struggling music student?

5   What's the verbal patter for counting eight strums per bar?

6   What's the verbal patter for counting 16ths?

Acoustic Guitar

7   What does '4/4' actually mean in music maths?

8   How much of the plectrum is it advisable to use to hit the strings?

9   What makes alternate picking so economical?

10 Where do you strike the strings if you want a mellow, sweet sound?

WEEK 7

Now we're going to start looking more closely at the subject of melody and where it comes from: scales. This is another vital area of music's superstructure that needs understanding from a student's point of view, and just a few minutes a day spent practising specific scales will aid your development considerably. Over the course of the week, we'll be looking at:

- The blues scale;

- The major scale;

- The minor scale;

- Pentatonic scales.

Acoustic Guitar

DAY 43: PLAYIN' THE BLUES

I think I've heard every excuse in the book for not practising scales, and I'll be the first to admit they're not the most inspiring or even most musical thing you can do when you have a guitar in your hands, but they *are* important: scales are to music what the alphabet is to written language – pretty fundamental and darned important, in other words. Scales can be imagined as the raw materials from which melodies are wrought. If

you want to be even more arty about it, you could say that they're like colours in a paintbox, each one a slightly different musical hue that combines with others to allow you to paint some really nice pictures.

PRACTICAL EXERCISE

What all this arty nonsense is leading us to, of course, is a week's worth of looking at scales, before you reach the 'graduation stage' in Week 8. It's an important leap into the machinery that makes music tick, and I want you to spend some time here really trying to take all of these sounds in. Don't worry, I'm not going to weigh you down with anything you really don't need to know. After all, there would be little point; it's in both our interests to cut to the chase as quickly as possible, so let's get on with proceedings straight away.

EXAMPLES

To give you an idea about how a scale can actually suggest the essential flavour of a music style, I'm going to begin our scalar sojourn with the briefest look at the blues.

Now, like it or not, the blues has probably had the most significant influence on modern music – fact. There are elements of blues in jazz, pop, country, heavy rock, nu-metal, you name it (apart, of course, from classical music; I haven't managed to detect an awful lot of blues in Bach).

Blues as a music form goes back further than many people believe. Despite the fact that blues wasn't recorded commercially until the 1920s, it was thriving in some form or other way before that time. As it developed and the musicians who played it migrated away from its birthplace in America's Deep South, it went on to form the foundation of popular music as we know it today. Without blues there would have been no Elvis Presley or Bill Haley, and possibly no Beatles, Rolling Stones or even Led Zeppelin, such is the extent of its influence.

But so much for history. What does this have to do with scales? Well, take a look at this example:

Track 36

First of all, play through the scale paying special attention to the tablature, because I want you to play it from the high notes to the low. (The reason why we're playing this particular scale backwards is because it sounds more reminiscent of blues and blues-influenced music this way around.) You'll notice that there are many open strings involved here, and this has the effect of making the job a little easier – it's only one fretted note per string, after all. Listen to the CD as a reference and guide.

You may be thinking to yourself that this doesn't sound too much like the blues, and you'd be right on two counts. Firstly, no scale sounds exactly like the music that has been derived from it, in the same way that the major scale (which we'll get to later in the week) doesn't sound like either the British National Anthem or

Beethoven's 'Ode To Joy', despite both melodies being based on it. Secondly, we're not quite finished with this particular scale yet...

Now that you've got a very basic idea about this scale, I'm going to add a couple of notes to it and make it sound a little more bluesy by turning it into a 'pseudo-lick':

Track 36

I think you'll agree, it sounds more like the blues – even if it still manages to fall short of everything that either Eric Clapton or Stevie Ray Vaughan have ever played!

DAY 43 STUDY

For today's study piece, I'm going to add the vital element of harmony to the blues scale you've just learned. Playing almost any series of single notes – ie a melody line – without the supporting harmony beneath it is only ever telling half the story, and so you should find that things begin to sound altogether more bluesy from this point on. Now take a look at the study piece over the page:

Acoustic Guitar

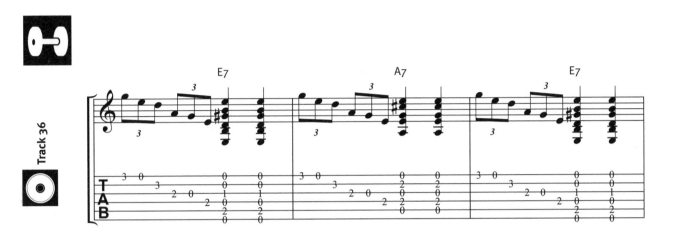

New chord –
take care!

Take things slowly here and make sure that you listen to the CD example as a guide.

DAY 44: A MAJOR INCIDENT

Yesterday's look at the blues was never destined to be anything more than a flavourful insight into the inner core of this all important music form. There's a lot more to it than merely learning one scale, as you probably imagined! In fact, I'm not here to influence you stylistically at all – that side of your playing will come from you. You'll doubtless have your own set of musical preferences that will count in some way towards the music you end up wanting to play. And once you've completed this guided tour and honed your technique a little more with practice, there'll be nothing to stop you from following your own course.

PRACTICAL EXERCISE

As we saw during yesterday's brief look at the blues, scales don't really represent anything terribly musical when played on their own, but they are invaluable from the point of view that you're getting your fingers used to the various musical highways and byways of the fretboard.

EXAMPLES

At seminars, I sometimes refer to something I call the *universal fretboard*, which is conceptualised thus: if you imagine that every great piece of music, guitar solo or whatever has been played on one single guitar fretboard, then by examining it and looking for the more 'well-trod' areas, you can begin to get an idea of where the common ground lies. By familiarising yourself with this, you'll be preparing yourself for most of what music can throw at you. And, of course, if this kind of thing is possible, it's doubtless that one scale in particular will show up as being in more common usage than any of the others: the major scale.

Acoustic Guitar

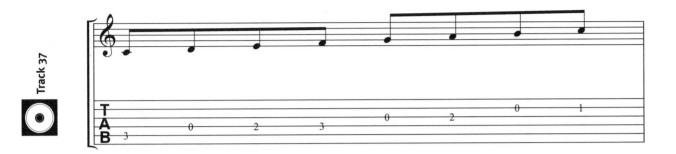

The major scale is hundreds of years old and has featured in all kinds of music from the Renaissance through to modern music (and that, if you're not aware already, covers a whole lot of ground!). Some of the greatest and most memorable melodies have been drawn from it – everything from Bach to James Taylor and beyond, in fact – so it's obviously something that you should become familiar with, and you need to do this in two distinctly different ways.

Firstly, your fingers must know it – and eventually it will become important for you to know it in every conceivable position on the guitar fretboard. (This will prepare your digits for most of the music journeying they will undertake in the future, after all.) And secondly, your ear has to become familiar with it; a good amount of musical expertise actually begins with having a set of ears that have been attuned to many of the inner devices that makes music work – and that job begins here.

In a perfect world, of course, this would happen naturally because, as you repeat the major scale by practising and learning it, your ear will absorb it at an almost unconscious level. (Incidentally, this is another reason why you should try to ensure that your practice time never becomes dull and repetitious. It's important that you remain alert so that you have the best possible chance to gain the maximum benefit.)

So, as far as the major scale is concerned, if you're using a plectrum, use alternate picking as before – if you're using your fingers, alternate between *i* and

195

Acoustic Guitar

m. Take it slowly – we're really not concerned with speed here; walking pace is fine – and try to make every note equal in duration. Remember that rhythm is one of the three vital areas to serve, musically speaking!

DAY 44 STUDY

As with yesterday's study piece, the flavour of a scale is only really evident when you hear it played in its natural environment – in this case, the corresponding major chord of C – so here I've constructed a little study interleaving the major chord, scale and arpeggio to hammer home the true extent to which all are interlinked. Watch out for both right- and left-hand markings here; you can fingerpick or use a plectrum (or why not try both?).

Track 37

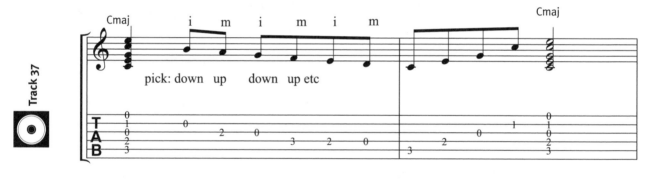

DAY 45: MINOR WORK AHEAD

You're probably aware that we live in a world of opposites: day and night, dark and light, sweet and sour, etc. The same kind of thing exists in music, too – part of the essential workings at music's centre is driven by the contrast between the sweet-sounding and the dissonant, for example. The opposite number to the major scale is the minor, and that's the scale we're going to look at today.

PRACTICAL EXERCISE

It might represent a little bit of a generalisation, but I suppose you could say that the principal difference in sound between major and minor scales is as simple as this: major scales sound happy and positive whereas the minor scales tend to sound sad and negative.

EXAMPLES

You need to hear the difference for yourself, of course, so here's the minor scale, which is to be played exactly as before (ie watch the tab and use alternate picking or fingers *i* and *m*):

Track 38

As it's very important that you're able to tell the difference between major and minor, here are both once again so that you can compare the two side by side:

Acoustic Guitar

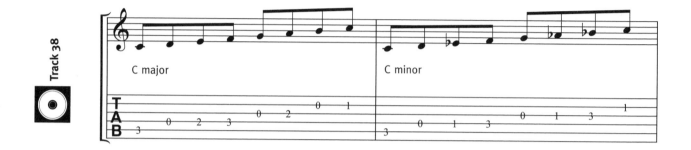

Track 38

C major

C minor

You'll probably agree with the definition above – there's definitely a difference, with the minor scale sounding sad and bitter against its major counterpart. This difference is carried over into chords, too, and here are a few shown side by side so you can compare them:

A major

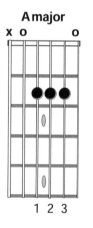

1 2 3

A minor

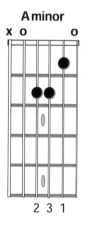

2 3 1

D major

1 3 2

D minor

2 3 1

E major

3 2 1

E minor

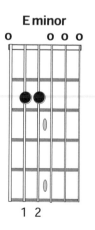

1 2

Acoustic Guitar

All you really have to do here is play each of the chords and listen hard. Your ear will be beginning to develop now, so there should be an obvious difference all round.

DAY 45 STUDY

Let's put the minor scale into the same kind of context as before, sitting it alongside its chord and arpeggio forms so that your ear really does receive the maximum minor-scale dose possible!

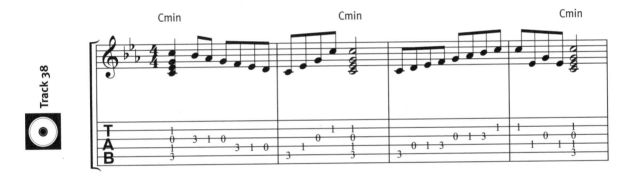

Incidentally, you'll notice that the chord of C minor is another awkward one. This is definitely a chord that assumes a fairly good span within the left hand, so don't be discouraged if, once again, it feels like you've hit a brick wall. Your hand is developing all the time, so try to follow the fingering shown in the tab. Things should work out eventually.

Acoustic Guitar

DAY 46: CLOSED-POSITION SCALES

So far, all the scales we've looked at this week have been down at the nut end of the fretboard and have employed open or unfretted strings. This type of scale is known as an *open-position scale*. But we obviously can't be locked down at this end of the guitar fretboard for ever, so we need to venture further up the fretboard, and this means learning a couple of *closed-position* scale shapes.

PRACTICAL EXERCISE

For today's exercise, first of all you'll need to compare a couple of different-looking scale shapes:

Track 39

If you play through both of these exercises one after the other, you might be surprised to find that they're identical. This is one of the guitar's stranger habits – there are quite a few places on the fretboard where you can play exactly the same thing! There's no cosmic reason as to why this should be so; it's just intrinsic to many stringed instruments, that's all. So it might appear that the guitar fretboard is absolutely festooned with notes, but in reality that's not the case.

If you want the maths (and I just know that you do) the average acoustic guitar has around 138 notes on it, but only 47 of them are unique pitches! So around

Acoustic Guitar

two-thirds of the guitar fretboard is covered with notes you can find elsewhere on the neck. If you think that this can make things confusing, you'd be dead right, but don't let it worry you. You just need to be aware of it at this stage, that's all.

EXAMPLES

Here are some more closed-position scales to look at. First, a couple of majors:

And now a couple of minors:

The directive here is to study the left-hand fingering for all of these scales before you begin to practise them in your daily routine. Whatever you do, don't leave things to chance and don't settle for a haphazard 'custom' fingering for them just because you think that your little finger isn't strong enough to perform them quite right just yet; it's vital to the development of both left and right hands that

Acoustic Guitar

they take these new challenges on board from the word go and that you don't shy away because you don't think they're up to the task. So please make sure that both hands are configured correctly before you begin the job of actually learning the scales – old habits, after all, die hard.

Track 39

DAY 46 STUDY

For today's study material, I've constructed a piece that starts off being major and ends up being minor. To begin with, look at the chord symbols above the music and play through these (the transition between keys is probably more obvious when you hear the chords in isolation), then work your way through the piece. Check what you're playing against the CD track to make sure everything is going well.

I've tried to keep everything as rhythmically simple as possible in this piece, but unfortunately there's no way I can write rhythm down for you without teaching you to read music first, and that's something that falls well beyond the scope of this book. Just try your best and use the CD for reference.

DAY 47: GOING PENTATONIC

That's a nice long word to start today's lesson: pentatonic. Don't panic – music is full of words like this. All *pentatonic* means is 'five note'.

There's a large number of five-note scales in music. On the whole they tend to reside more in folk music than anywhere else. However, don't think of the 'folk' tradition as such being all real ale and fol-de-ra; I tend to use the term in its broadest sense, to cover just about everything that isn't thought of as being at all institutionalised or learned formally. Folk music has the tradition of being passed down from generation to generation in the form of an *aural tradition* – in other words, it's not written down or learnt academically; it's taught to successive generations by ear.

Taking this definition on board, it's possible to think of blues, jazz and other blues-related music as being, to some extent, folk. You could even argue that rock 'n' roll has something of the folk tradition about it, in the manner in which it's composed. But, whatever the case, pentatonic (or five-note) scales abound in folk music the world over; virtually every culture on the globe has a pentatonic scale at the heart of its folk music – and that includes places as diverse as Japan and Scotland!

We've actually met up with a pentatonic scale already. Remember this?

Track 40

Acoustic Guitar

Before we messed with it in order to bend it slightly towards the blues, this particular scale started off as something known in music circles as the *minor pentatonic scale*. And, as with the other scales in this series, there are more places to play this particular scale than down at the nut; there are several 'closed' positions for the minor pentatonic, too, and it's these we'll look at first:

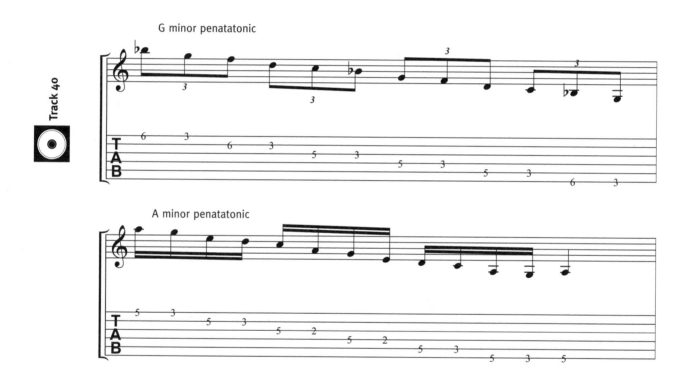

I'm not going to weigh you down with all five of the closed-position shapes for this particular scale, because we're not really here to undertake a course in learning scale positions. What I do want to do, however, is introduce you to the sound of the scale in a couple of positions on the fretboard so that your ear has the best possible chance of picking up on its sound.

Make sure that you follow the tablature on this one – it's vital with playing scales that you begin and end on the right notes. Otherwise the sound of the scale will

be blurred and you won't be achieving the objective of introducing your ear to these important new sounds.

DAY 47 STUDY

To round off today's lesson, here's a workout for the minor pentatonic scale that will test your picking (plectrum or fingers) and co-ordination skills:

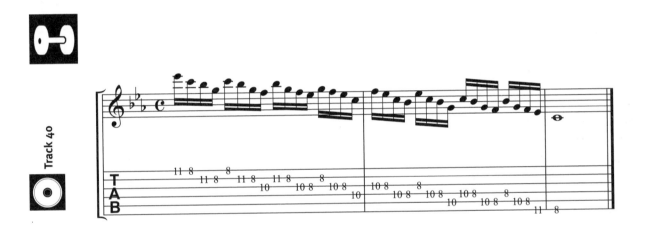

Take your time with it, as usual, and try to ensure that everything is cleanly picked and rhythmically spaced. If you have any doubts, listen to the CD!

Acoustic Guitar

DAY 48: MAJOR PENTATONICS

As I said back on Day 45, everything (well, nearly everything) in music has a counterpart that tends to represent its opposite. Just as there are both major and minor scales, there are also major and minor pentatonic scales.

PRACTICAL EXERCISE

When we compared the major and minor scales together a couple of days ago, we found that there was a distinct contrast between the two. The same is true here, between the two pentatonic scales – but in some ways there are more similarities.

EXAMPLES

Have a look at the following example:

C major pentatonic

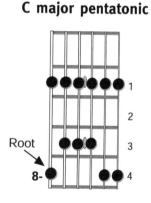

C minor pentatonic

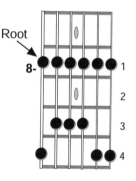

It won't take you long to spot exactly what I mean about similarities. It's not a misprint, the two shapes are the same; they're just positioned differently on the guitar neck. So this lesson doesn't really rely on you learning much in the way of new material; it's mainly down to listening, once again. Let's look at another couple of positions:

D minor pentatonic

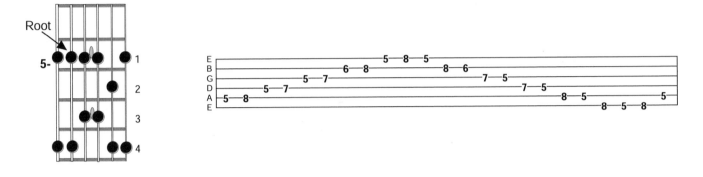

D major pentatonic

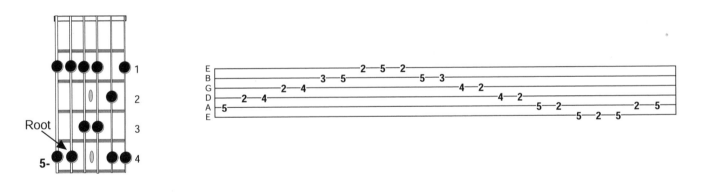

Once again, minor and major shapes are identical at first glance, but the
fretboard locations and tablature are different.

DAY 48 STUDY

Today's study piece does the job of placing the major and minor pentatonic
scales in their proper surroundings to give you the best chance of hearing the
contrast between them. Take note of the fingering in the tab and make sure that
you're spot on every time.

Acoustic Guitar

You'll be delighted – and possibly a little surprised – to hear that this is about it as far as scales are concerned, at least for the time being. Of course, there are many more scales hiding in the recesses of music's vast wardrobe, but we don't have to bother with them quite yet. What I've given you here will be sufficient to get your fingers working and begin the serious job of developing your ears without the need to dig any deeper.

Acoustic Guitar

DAY 49

WEEK 7 TEST

Time for your penultimate test. This one's designed to determine what you've picked up on the subject of the blues, as well as major and minor and open- and closed-position scales.

1 Where is the blues's birthplace?

2 Scales are to music what the _____ is to language. (Fill in the blank.)

3 What's the most common scale in music?

4 What's one of the principal benefits of repeating scale exercises?

5 Sweet/sour, dark/light, up/down major/_____?

6 What's the difference between closed- and open-position scales?

Acoustic Guitar

7 How many unique pitches are there on the guitar neck?

8 What does the word *pentatonic* actually mean?

9 Name the four scales you looked at this week.

10 Pentatonic scales can be found only in blues – true or false?

WEEK 8

It's graduation time! This is our final week together, so over the next seven days I'll be putting everything we've looked at together so far into one basic package. I'm going to tell you how to take all the individual elements of your basic music technique further by outlining practice routines and suggestions for further study.

As I said at the beginning of the book, the objective of *Crash Course Acoustic Guitar* is to give you enough information for you to establish some basic technique and rudimentary music skills so that you can venture out on your own and begin to choose your own direction, style and general taste in the music you play.

Acoustic Guitar

DAY 50: CHORDS

This is pretty much where we came in! Over the course of the book, you've learned many of the common chords that you'll find in music books and songbooks everywhere. I couldn't prepare you for everything, obviously, but I hope that I can set you on the right path for some further study over the next couple of pages.

All of the chords we've looked at so far fall into those three family groups that I told you about earlier: majors, minors and sevenths. You could say that these are the more everyday chords that you'll come across most often in music and songbooks, but naturally there are many more chords out there, and you're going to find that you keep running into examples that you're not familiar with.

! There's not really any way that you can prepare yourself for this in advance, either – experience is definitely the best teacher in this respect. The important thing is that the work we've done so far with chord shapes in this book will equip you for channelling the new and unfamiliar chords into your playing. The mechanics of playing chords – literally the everyday task of placing flesh on fretboard and getting a decent sound out of your instrument – has already been done, so you should find that you can assimilate any new information in this area quite quickly.

The best thing to do here is to buy a good chord book and keep it handy for reference (if you haven't done so already). Then, whenever you come across a shape that you haven't met before, look it up and write it down somewhere. Then adopt it in your practice routine to give you a good chance of remembering it for next time. This way, your repertoire of chord shapes and names will keep on growing until you know pretty much all of the ones that are common to whichever style of music you play.

It's important to have a good knowledge of basic majors, minors and sevenths in every key – that's three for each of these 12-letter names:

Acoustic Guitar

A	A♯/B♭	B	C	C♯/D♭	D	D♯/E♭	E	F	F♯/G♭	G	G♯/A♭
1	2	3	4	5	6	7	8	9	10	11	12

If it sounds like a lot of work, you're right, it is – and it's true that some of the chords are in more common use than others. Favourite keys and chords tend to be dictated by each and every instrument; on the piano, for instance, the easiest key is C major, while on the sax it's B♭ and on the guitar it's E, A, D and G, because those keys all contain user-friendly chords. But out there in the real world, you're probably going to be playing songs that were originally written for different instruments or singers with particular vocal ranges, so it's best to be as prepared as possible.

EXAMPLES

By far the easiest way of covering the work outlined above is by becoming familiar with the principle of playing barre chords. We've looked a little at this already, and you're doing really well if your hand has developed the necessary muscle after only seven and a bit weeks' study. But you know my theory in this respect: begin the work now for use later on when you discover you need it. Here are three barre-chord shapes to look at:

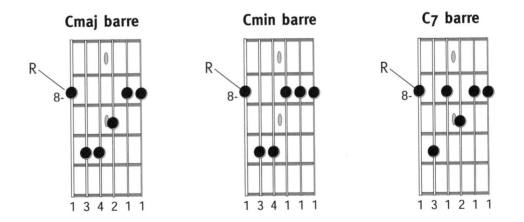

These are going to be real handfuls to begin with – as I said, the muscles in your left hand probably won't have had chance to develop enough as yet – but be patient because learning to play barre chords will save you an awful lot of work in the future.

Acoustic Guitar

The first thing to do with each is lay the first finger across the fretboard and make sure you've got a good 'lock' on the strings – that is, a good, clear note out of each individual string. Next, place the fingers one at a time, constantly checking that each string is still ringing clear. If it is, then all's well and good. If not, round up the usual suspects – check the thumb position, make sure the fingers are playing on their tips as much as possible and not sitting across two strings instead of one, etc.

Once each chord is basically working, hold it for a few seconds at a time. Take your fingers off the neck and then replace them to test again whether or not you've got a good sound. Repeat this exercise several times during your practice routine and you'll soon find these chords becoming easier and easier.

DAY 50 STUDY

Here's a chord arrangement that has a single barre chord in its midst. This will give you a chance to put your barre playing to the test, as we'll apply exactly the same rules as before – that is, we don't want any bumps in the road where it takes you longer to lay the barre than it does to play any of the other chords.

B minor barre

D basic major

G major

A7

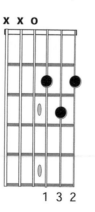

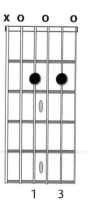

Acoustic Guitar

| B minor / / / | Dmaj / / / | Gmaj / / / | A7 / / / ||

Use the piece shown on the previous page as a meter to gauge how your barre playing is progressing – and remember to vary the strum rhythms and include some dynamics along the way!

Acoustic Guitar

DAY 51: LIFE BEHIND BARRES

Today we're going to continue our look at barre chords and see how we can use this new information to give us a concise and useful grasp of all the common chords in one fell swoop.

PRACTICAL EXERCISE

I've already given you three shapes for barre chords: one major, one minor and one seventh. Today, we're going to look at one more shape for each to ensure that we've got this basic chord idea wrapped up. Here are the next three shapes to look at:

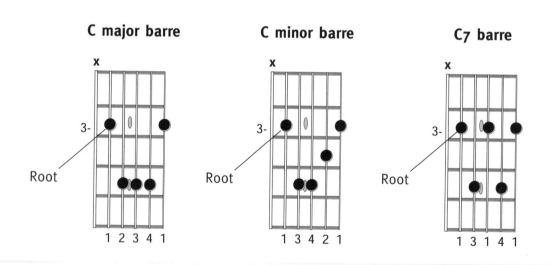

If anything, you might find that the major chord shape is the most difficult to get your fingers around at first. Believe it or not, the more common way of fingering this particular chord shape is like this:

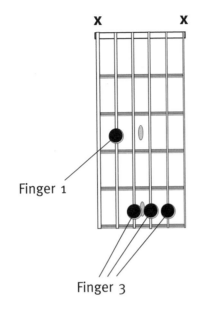

Finger 1

Finger 3

It might seem impossible at first, but the third finger does actually become flexible enough to hold down these three strings together!

Try it by all means, but it's my bet that your third finger isn't quite ready for the type of gymnastics required to play it. Remember what I said about the joints of the fingers becoming more and more flexible as time goes on? Well, this particular barre shape is a pretty good demonstration of that. However, if you check back every so often, you'll find that you'll be able to adopt this fingering after a while.

EXAMPLES

You'll have noticed a little arrow with the letter 'R' pointing to the lowest notes of all of the six barre shapes you've come across so far. This stands for *root*, and it's going to help us to expand the barre-chord system to its fullest extent.

Because all of these shapes employ the first finger to lock off all of the strings – that is, there are no open strings in any of the chords – we can actually employ them all over the fretboard. This is what I mean when I say that using barre chords is the most efficient way of making sure that you have those basic chords covered on the fretboard. Learn these six shapes, then learn how to move them around a bit and *voilà*! Job done. In other words, played at this point on the neck, this chord shape gives us G major:

Acoustic Guitar

G barre

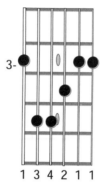

Moved up a few frets, the same shape will give us C major:

C barre

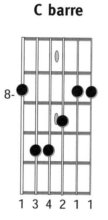

So it's pretty much a case of one chord shape equalling 12 major chords. The only blank we need to fill in now is exactly where to find them all. With this in mind, take a look at the diagram at the top of the next page:

Acoustic Guitar

E A D G B E

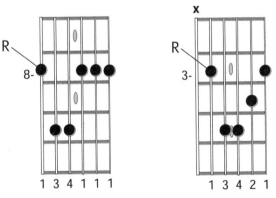

Basically, what you have here is a map of the fretboard showing you where all of the notes on the two bass strings lie. Now, you see all those lines pointing to the Rs below? All you have to do is line them up on the appropriate note and you've got an instant chord. In other words, if you were looking for C minor (remember how difficult that was to play down at the nut?), all you'd need to do would be to find a convenient C on either the E or A strings and play the major barre shape there, like this:

C minor barres

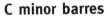

And if you wanted a G7, you'd apply the same logic:

G7 barres

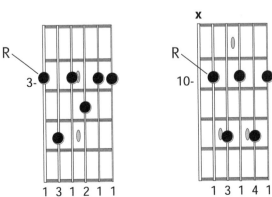

Acoustic Guitar

So you should be able to see now how useful the barre-chord system is once you've got used to it.

DAY 51 STUDY

Now, this will involve a little bit of writing on your part, but today I suggest that you copy out the neck chart on the previous page and keep it with your guitar – in its case or bag, for example. Be sure to make it bigger than the one in the book so that it's easier to read from a distance (ie when you have your guitar in your hands). Take it from me, you're going to need it!

For today's study piece, I want you to find these chords and try to play their barre versions:

- Amin
- D7
- E7
- Fmaj
- Amaj
- C7
- Bmin

Either of the two shapes available for each will do. You can check to see if you're at the correct fret location by playing the 'open' chord positions you learned earlier on in the course. If the two sound like a match, then all's well. If not, go back and check your figures to find out where you slipped up.

If you keep this exercise in your practice routine for a few days, you'll find that you'll soon begin to remember where the notes are on the strings. At that point, just write out some random letters from the music alphabet (ie A–G) and try to find major, minor and seventh chords for each of them.

DAY 52: PICKING PERFECTION

So far you've done a fair amount of work with a plectrum in your right hand, but the chances are that it still might occasionally feel a little awkward or cumbersome. A few students have compared learning to use a pick with learning to use chopsticks, and I guess that I can see some kind of similarity.

PRACTICAL EXERCISE

In order to get your picking up to a good level of proficiency, you're going to need some sort of workout in your practice routine that has the effect of buffing your developing skills in this area to a shine. It would be true to say that you don't necessarily need to go too crazy with your pick training; electric-guitar players need to do some considerable work in this area to be able to perform some of the aerobatics that feature in modern rock-guitar playing, but we acoustic players are altogether a more refined bunch in this respect, I think you'll agree!

EXAMPLES

In order to survive in the plectrum-wielding world at large, your skills need to develop in three essential areas: playing melodies, chords and arpeggios. A good level of competence in all three will prepare you for all but the lunatic fringe of acoustic-guitar playing. So how do you go about improving in these key areas? Read on...

Your first task is to take a scale fragment like the one at the top of the next page and slowly increase your picking speed in general:

Acoustic Guitar

Alternate picking throughout

Track 43

If you have a metronome (and for this kind of exercise a metronome is a good thing to have handy, so put it on your Christmas list), start off at a slow beat of around 60, playing one note per click. If you haven't got a metronome handy, a loudly ticking clock might give you a reference for 60 beats per minute (ie one note per second).

When you're sure that you can play the scale fragment at 60 beats per minute without stopping, fluffing or playing any wrong notes, increase the speed of the metronome to 66 and try again.

Increase the speed of the click gradually – no leaps, please; impatience won't get you anywhere – and repeat the process. When you reach 120 beats per minute, go back to 60 and play two notes per click (it should be exactly the same as one note at 120) and begin the process all over again. Aim to reach two notes at 120bpm – a good, useful speed to be getting on with.

DAY 52 STUDY

Some more exercises that will increase your facility with a plectrum include those featured over the page:

Alternate pick strokes on every note

Each of them should take its place in your practice routine with the same sort of guidelines as before. Use a metronome to increase gradually the rate and speed at which you're picking the strings. Take things dead slow – we're still laying foundations here, and they have to be solid before we can consider building anything else on top.

Acoustic Guitar

DAY 53: ARPEGGIOS

We've already looked at strumming patterns – the most common way of accompanying a song – and developing a keen sense of rhythm here is the key to progress in this department. Working with a metronome will do wonders for your rhythm playing – there are no grey areas here: it will work; it always does. In order to be able to split a basic beat into mathematically equal parts, your understanding of the fundamentals has to be fully attuned, so any work you can do toward becoming more aware of music's pulse is worthwhile.

In essence, it's experience that will teach you the most in the strumming department from now on. Working through songbooks and accompanying yourself or your friends can do nothing but add to your learning experience, and you're bound to discover many of the accepted methods of accompaniment as you progress. However, playing arpeggios – with a plectrum as opposed to fingers – is another area entirely…

PRACTICAL EXERCISE

Any arpeggio played with a plectrum is going to stretch the facilities of the right hand significantly. There's a lot of movement involved, and hence a greater margin for error. Just remind yourself how much movement is involved in playing this arpeggio, based on the C major chord:

Alternate picking throughout

Acoustic Guitar

Hopefully you'll see what I mean, and yet you'll probably agree that it's an effective and quite attractive method for accompaniment. As most of the errors tend to lie within the domain of accurate string selection, adopting a simple workout that focuses on this one task should set you on the correct path.

EXAMPLES

Let's take a basic arpeggio-accompaniment training programme and work from the ground up. First of all, imagine that you've never done any work in this area at all and begin with open-string work. Remember that the most effective way of channelling this kind of information into the brain is by ridding yourself of as many distracting variables as possible. This is true in virtually all problems associated with playing guitar – most can be cured by stripping them right back to a very basic level, as this is often where the real bugs are to be found. Even now, after playing for many, many years, I often make myself go back a few steps and look at things from a fresh perspective to see if I can make a particular element any stronger. It usually pays off, too...

So what's going to feature in our arpeggio workout? Like I say, begin with a few open-string exercises like these:

Track 44

Acoustic Guitar

All you're doing here is varying the order in which you're playing the open strings, giving yourself a chance to make sure that the pick is tracking correctly on the strings.

Now, I want you to be really strict with yourself here and not try to go any further before all of these open-string exercises are note-perfect. Moving on too soon will leave a weakness in your playing that will come back to haunt you later on. Just remember that tall buildings need strong foundations.

Next we'll take a few chords and arpeggiate them, in much the same way that we did while looking at fingerstyle playing:

Track 44

Acoustic Guitar

Take each chord individually and, once again, spend some time on it until you're
sure that everything is locked down.

For today's study, we're going to take what we've been learning with regard to
plectrum arpeggios and put them into some kind of context.

Track 44

Acoustic Guitar

This exercise probably won't sound too great the first time you play it through –
and that's why it will have to remain on the practice workbench for some time.
I've tried to keep the chords as simple as possible because it's the right hand
that has to cover all the new territory, but, as with anything, you can expect quite
a few slip-ups whilst you're getting things up and running.

Once all the chords are basically working, play them against a metronome to
make sure that your timing is spot on. Keep things slow at first and work up to
speed gradually.

DAY 54: FINGERSTYLE FINISHING SCHOOL

By now your finger-picking skills should be taking shape nicely. We've done some work here in the past few weeks to the extent that we even began to combine melody and bass together at one point. The objective now, though, is to ensure that you can fingerpick your way through an accompaniment pretty much flawlessly. You'll never be ready for everything music can throw at you (none of us are!), but you can at least aim to make sure that you're fully equipped with all of the essential tools in this area.

PRACTICAL EXERCISE

Once again, the way to solve all of your fingerstyle teething troubles is to address things at a very basic level and work up. If things are still a little lumpy, go back to the first exercises we looked at, on open strings, and make sure that they're working as well as they should be.

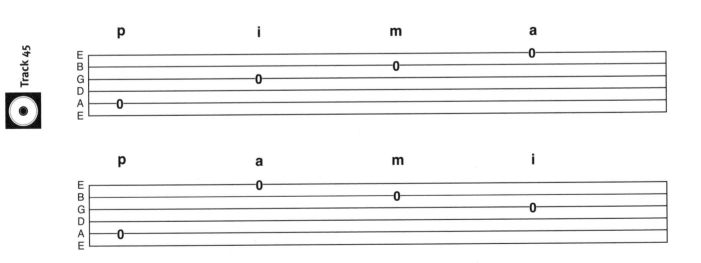

Don't be prepared to let anything second-rate pass quality control here. Your version of these exercises have got to be as good as the one on the CD. No excuses!

Acoustic Guitar

We've looked at the fundamentals of playing in time with fingerstyle, too, but not every accompaniment idea is necessarily going to be as perfectly symmetrical as the ones we've seen so far.

In the above example, you've got a kind of circular movement going on in that your fingers travel across the strings and return to the position that they started in, ready to begin the 'circle' once again. This needn't always be the case, however, as in these excerpts:

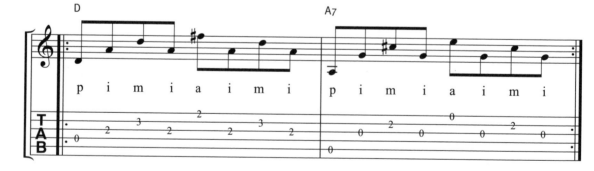

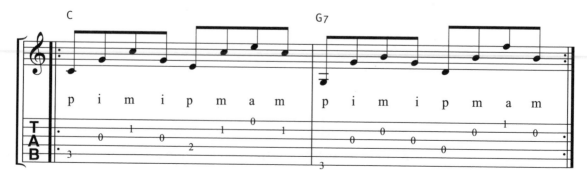

230

Or it might even be something of a mix-and-match situation between fingerstyle
and strumming:

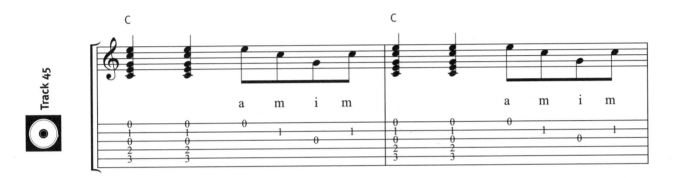

There might even be some melodic movement involved, too:

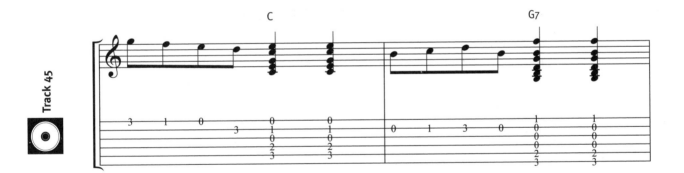

In short, there are many, many variations upon the basic idea of fingerstyle, but
all centre around a few core principles – for example, a right-hand fingering
'system' based on the thumb looking after strings 4, 5 and 6 while the fingers
tend to be assigned *i* = third, *m* = second and *a* = first.

Economy of movement is important, too. (Remember the trigger-finger principle,
where the finger returns to its original 'ready to pluck' position naturally, without
having to be consciously relocated?) Don't let the right-hand fingers wander too
far away from the strings; flamboyant gesturing is all well and good on the

concert platform, but in the practice chamber discipline rules. Remember that economy of movement has to be developed by both hands in order to make each movement as efficient as possible.

Once again, experience will be a great teacher here – songbooks and transcriptions will lead you further down the path towards fingerstyle enlightenment. If you hear something on a recording and you want to know how it was done, the chances are that there's a readily available transcription somewhere, and you should be able to locate it after a couple of minutes' searching on the internet.

DAY 54 STUDY

I've constructed a little fingerstyle study for you here that you should keep in your practice routine for a while. My advice here is the same as always: take things slowly, a little at a time. Don't try to play through the whole piece and end up disappointed when it hiccups and splutters to a stop. And make sure that all the component parts are working before you attempt a performance, even if it means working through things one bar at a time. The whole thing is shown over the page:

Acoustic Guitar

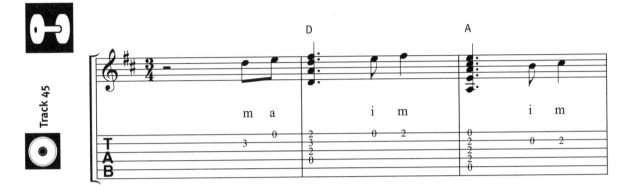

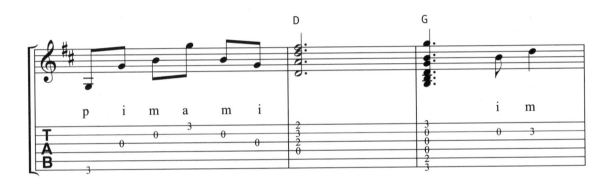

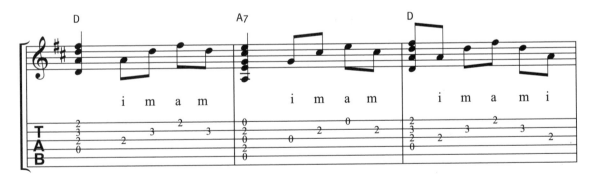

Acoustic Guitar

DAY 55: THE FUTURE

The aim for this last lesson is to put everything together. By taking on board everything covered today, you'll be able to take your playing even further all by yourself.

SEEK GUIDANCE

The first piece of advice would be to consider finding a teacher who will continue to pace you by introducing you to new material and as many of the variations in song-playing technique as possible. So many people have found that their playing has improved dramatically after a few months with a teacher.

DON'T BE A HERMIT!

Guitarists are renowned for being solitary animals, and it doesn't do us much good. Once again, virtually everyone I've ever taught has confirmed that their playing has undergone a positive metamorphosis when they began playing with other people. It doesn't have to be anything too formal or daunting, like a jam session; simply finding someone – or, indeed, a few people – looking to make music together will be fine. The main advantages here are that you can learn from each other, and you'll doubtless be led into different stylistic areas.

It's a well-known fact that choice of repertoire is a democratic process in duos or bands, and this inevitably results in you being exposed to material you're not familiar with, which is very good for you. Basically, any time spent with a guitar in your hands and playing anything will be of benefit to you at this stage.

KEEP UP THE PRACTICE ROUTINE

By now, you should have found that practising has become a habit to the extent that you actually miss it if it doesn't happen. (I used to be absolutely guilt-ridden if I missed my daily routine. No, seriously, I did!) With this discipline in place, it should be easy to keep the momentum that we've established together up and running. Remember that a good, orderly practice workbench will be of benefit to

you throughout all stages of your playing career. We all keep learning, no matter how far we think we've taken our playing. The guitar is just that kind of instrument – it's almost impossible to know everything about it.

BECOME YOUR OWN ANALYST

If something's not working right in your playing, there's only one thing that will put it right: practice. However, knowing exactly what's wrong and how to put it right might be down to you to sort out and diagnose (especially if you don't have a teacher). Virtually every problem will fall into one of two categories – musical or technical – and you might find that it's down to you to identify which.

To simplify the process a little, you could say that a musical problem might be something like an unfamiliar chord – all you need to do is go and look it up and it's solved. But if that chord has awkward fingering – a big stretch or a difficult barre, for instance – then it becomes a technical problem. You see the distinction?

Being able to diagnose and treat problems that players come across in this way is familiar territory for a teacher – it's a skill you soon learn – but being able to self-diagnose is invaluable. Remember that any problem, no matter how slight, can be addressed with a carefully wrought practice plan.

DO SOME EAR TRAINING

A musician's ears are his or her greatest ally. Having a good musical ear is something that's useful way beyond just being able to tell that your guitar is either in or out of tune. Properly trained, it can identify chords and chord sequences, pick out melodies from records and much more. However, few people come to music with this skill already up and running.

Ear training is an area that's often ignored or not maintained by students. Some believe that it comes as part of the general 'package deal' of learning to play. It doesn't. You've already seen in this book that the only sure-fire way of improving any element of your playing is by isolating it and focusing on it exclusively, and

this applies to ear training, too. Luckily, there are now many ways whereby a good degree of skill can be developed quite easily. It can even become fun!

If you have a computer and access to the internet (and I'm guessing that you probably do), run a quick search for 'ear training' and you'll doubtless come up with many programs that have been designed to drill musicians in the art. Many of them are very gradual, starting off by getting you to identify intervals (ie scale notes), with the computer playing you two notes from a scale and asking you to tell it what they are (sounds harder than it is, believe me!). With most, you can graduate their skill levels so that you begin by identifying only chord tones and work up to identifying the different types of scale.

All of that lies in the future, though. For now, download one and have a play with it – treat it like a game. You'll find yourself absorbing some important information almost unconsciously.

Apart from that, the most important thing you can do while you continue playing is remember to listen to everything you do. Don't dismiss something because you've played it 100 times before; keep listening. The music will begin to suggest things to you. Play it slightly differently, louder, softer, and you can make an enormous difference.

KEEP AN OPEN MIND

This is possibly the hardest thing to do, but it's certainly one of the most valuable. Never dismiss anything out of hand; always try to see its musical value. Keep your learning as broad-based as possible – I've surprised many hard-rock students in the past by introducing them to some techniques associated with a style other than their own. You can learn so much from keeping those ears open, and everything you hear will go towards enriching your enjoyment and general experience of playing music.

Acoustic Guitar

AND FINALLY...

If anything in this book is troubling you, feel free to contact me via email at www.davidmead.net. There's a link there for you to email me direct, and I answer every one I get. Promise!

Acoustic Guitar

DAY 56

WEEK 8 TEST

Well, here it is, your final test. This isn't included here to catch you out, but neither, if you ace it, does it mean that you know everything about playing guitar. It's here as a guide – nothing more, nothing less. So no cheating!

1   How do different instruments define their own common keys?

2   How many chords do you need to know as a 'starter pack'?

3   What does the letter *R* mean in relation to barre-chord shapes?

4   What is the overwhelming convenience associated with learning to play barre chords properly?

5   Where do most errors occur with plectrum arpeggio playing?

6   What's to be gained from reviewing the basics in your playing every so often?

7   Why should you not let the fingers wander too far from the strings in a fingerpicking piece?

8   What's the value of seeking out a teacher to help you further your studies?

9   What's the difference between a musical and a technical guitar problem?

10 One note per beat at 120 beats per minute is equal to two at 60 – true or false?

03/12 (182413)